D1439134

THE
CONCEPT OF ECONOMIC CO-OPERATION
IN SOUTHERN AFRICA

The
Concept of Economic Co-operation in Southern Africa

by

J. A. LOMBARD
Professor in Economics, University of Pretoria

J. J. STADLER
Associate Professor in Economics, University of Pretoria

P. J. VAN DER MERWE
Senior lecturer in Economics, University of Pretoria

for

Bureau for Economic Policy and Analysis, Pretoria

PUBLICATION NO. 1

Published by

ECONBURO (PTY.) LIMITED
P.O. Box 2393 PRETORIA
Available in the USA from Richard Abel & Co. Inc.

CONTENTS

BUREAU FOR ECONOMIC POLICY AND ANALYSIS

The objectives of the Bureau are:–

• to serve public opinion in regard to the daily acts of government so as to enable households and businesses to judge more articulately and intelligently the past, current and future actions of government in economic affairs; and

• to promote sound principles of political economy in South African affairs.

ASSOCIATES

Prof. J. A. Lombard, University of Pretoria (Convenor)
Prof. J. J. N. Cloete, University of Pretoria
Prof. F. J. du Plessis, University of Pretoria
Prof. D. P. Erasmus, Potchefstroom University for C.H.E.
Prof. D. W. Goedhuys, University of South Africa
Prof. C. F. Nieuwoudt, University of Pretoria
Prof. D. J. G. Smith, University of Orange Free State
Prof. J. J. Stadler, University of Pretoria
Prof. S. J. Terreblanche, University of Stellenbosch
Prof. F. van den Bogaerde, University of South Africa
Mr. P. J. van der Merwe, University of Pretoria
Mr. J. C. van Zyl, University of Pretoria
Prof. M. Wiechers, University of South Africa
Prof. A. P. Zevenbergen, University of Pretoria

The Bureau pursues its objectives through research and the expression of opinion in a variety of publications. This publication is the first of a series of broadsheets.

PREFACE

This booklet is concerned with the problem of the peaceful co-existence of different nations in Southern Africa. Our approach consists mainly of an effort to discuss the problem and the targets for policy in terms of population pressures, the geographic distribution of employment opportunities, and the limitations on the growth of employment opportunities in backward areas. Thus defined, these problems are neither unique nor novel. They have been the focal points of economics and other social sciences since the second world war, and have been among the practical determinants of international diplomacy.

In Southern Africa, however, these problems have been of more crucial importance than in most other parts of the world. On this sub-continent, the pressure of emigration from economically stagnant areas upon the social life of economically more dynamic communities has for decades been the overwhelming practical problem. North America and Europe, Australia and New Zealand are still protected from such invasions of other cultures by the cost of covering the greater distances, but in a number of cases, particularly the United States, the United Kingdom and Australia, a marginal taste of this problem has been offered.

On the whole, however, the international relationships between most of the developed countries on the one hand, and under-developed countries on the other hand, are more vaguely motivated than in Southern Africa. It is here, that we have to live daily with the problems of different nationalities pressing very hard on each other and on the available natural resources. In seeking a *modus vivendi* South Africa is developing a pattern of relationships which we propose to call *systematic co-operation*, and which may be looked upon as a clear alternative to *isolation* on the one hand, and *integration* on the other hand. The idea of systematic co-operation is to obtain the best of both worlds of politics and economics respectively, or perhaps more reasonably, to obtain the optimum combination of political independence and economic viability for the various culturally homogeneous population groups. The idea of this clear third alternative will be a prevailing one throughout the following pages.

9

To repeat: any idea of completely isolating the various cultural groups from each other must be rejected mainly on economic grounds – it would simply lead to starvation for most of them – while the idea of integration is rejected on the grounds of more purely cultural values and is consequently politically unacceptable.

The preparation of this publication was motivated by a number of stimulating public debates on this matter held during 1967 – debates in which the Department of Economics of the University of Pretoria took a leading part. Particularly the SABRA conference in Johannesburg in June, 1967, and the AIESEC conference in Pretoria in April, 1967, should be mentioned.

The public debate is continuing in 1968, fired by several imaginative (and occasionally also less encouraging) practical steps towards economic co-operation by the Republican Government. This publication is offered to the public in the hope that it may stimulate this discussion still further.

We believe that we have presented a straight-forward economic approach to the problem. We have not avoided economic concepts such as "comparative advantage", "linkage effects" etc., but we have tried to avoid unnecessary sophistication of economic arguments. This is not a text-book for students in economics only.

We should like to gratefully acknowledge the assistance of several persons and institutions who provided data required, in particular, the Africa Institute in Pretoria. A special word of thanks is also due to Messrs. C. J. Meintjes and J. M. Pieterse, assistants in the Department of Economics of the Pretoria University, for the spade work done by them under great pressure.

CHAPTER I

THE NATURE AND SIZE OF THE PROBLEM

1. *The nature of the problem*

In its broadest, somewhat philosophical, perspective, the problem
to be discussed in the following pages arises from two fundamental
aspects of the various peoples of Southern Africa. The first concerns their numbers; the second their aspirations. Neither their
numbers nor their aspirations would, in isolation, be problematic.
There is no absolute problem of population pressure on this sub-
continent, particularly if compared with the massive problems
in some parts of Asia. Neither would the aspirations to be discussed below, be a problem at all if it happened to collectively embrace the entire population irrespective of its numerical size and
composition.

The number of the Southern African population is a complex
number, in the sense that it cannot be envisaged realistically as
a single figure – its composition is an essential part of its meaning.
No individual in Southern Africa regards himself simply as a
member of the 45 million people living on the sub-continent. He
sees himself essentially as a member of a smaller group within
this total.

Thus our problem arises from the combination of these numbers
and their ideas. This combination need not, of course, necessarily
give rise to serious problems. As long as the ideas of the several
basic groups operate complementary, conflict does not arise. The
ideas of a buyer and a seller, respectively, normally result in a
mutually advantageous contract, but the ideas of two buyers
normally conflict. This does not mean that no reasonable solution
exists, but it means that a problem has to be solved.

In general, when aspirations become competitive, conflict arises
and solutions have to be sought. This, unfortunately, is the case
with the idea of individualism, the idea of separate families, and
finally the idea of separate nations and nationalism. We have to
belabour this point somewhat, for we hope to lead the reader to
the more practical issues of the problem without forever returning
to these premises.

If the idea of nationalism had collectively embraced all 45

million odd people on the sub-continent of Southern Africa, it would, of course, have operated completely complementary, but the simple fact is that it does not exist in this dimension.

Positive thinking compels us to regard as facts the collective actions of homogeneous groups all over Africa and indeed elsewhere, to identify themselves as separate units of collective decision making. In Europe the values of nationalism have in the past proved extremely strong motivational factors. They contained the ambitions of the Roman Church and confounded the ideas of the Habsburg emperors. Today, these values still constitute the most effective resistance in Eastern Europe against the dominance of international communism. In Africa nationalism is still in its infancy and need not necessarily follow the same pattern as in Europe. Loyalty often does not yet extend much further than tribal contexts, and the experiences in the Congo and Nigeria tend to indicate that a national state cannot simply arise from any random set of tribes.

Moreover, the fact that of the more than fifty separate political entities in the new Africa only thirteen have a population of more than 5 million people, seems to suggest that the "dark continent" may be carrying the process of political differentiation too far. We do not know, and it would be extremely difficult at the present stage of the development of political science to find, an unequivocal and absolute criterion of the optimum extent of political differentiation in social systems. The fact remains, as Colin Legum of the *London Observer* put it: "All the short term interests of the new African States favour nationalism". This idea of nationalism in Africa does not deny the identity of the white man at least as a separate "tribe", and indeed as a "white nation". Statements of many prominent black leaders support this view strongly. What does generate the fervent hate of the Black nationalist is "white" domination, whether from white South Africans or any other quarter.

Whatever our feelings may be about nationalism, we are not going to solve any problems in Africa by trying to either ignore its existence or to eliminate it, and we may be making a mistake to assume that it is on balance an undesirable force.

As the colonial powers of Europe rapidly withdrew their administrative control over African territories during this sixth decade of the twentieth century, and as 33 independent territories came into existence alongside 18 other separate territories, an interesting principle in socio-economic evolution was illustrated. This principle holds that a process of differentiation of a randomly assembled community into smaller more homogeneous social systems is a necessary precondition for the successful integration of these entities on a higher plane at a later stage. *In order to integrate successfully, one must first learn to differentiate properly.*

Neither could the problem be solved by removing the problem of numbers – e.g. by liquidation! When this problem is discussed among white South Africans (the numerically dominant group in the heartland of the Republic of South Africa – the Southern Transvaal) misguided references are occasionally made to the kind of solution the early North Americans and Australians were said to have adopted in their handling of the aboriginal "problem". This solution is contrasted with the opposite effect of the white settlement in the South African interior during the middle of the previous century when the regiments of the Zulu Napoleon, Chaka, had systematically been liquidating the smaller tribes scattered around them. With the arrival of the white pioneers (the Voortrekkers) these smaller tribes gained the latters' protection, and under the newly established balance of power, the birth rate among the Bantu peoples could again stand some chance of exceeding the death rate, which it soon did.

Thus the liquidation, in the previous century, of some of the Bantu tribes in Southern Africa was prevented and their development into different nations made possible.

Today, in the twentieth century, the liquidation of the white man in Southern Africa is often mentioned among some militants, but the idea seems equally misguided. Apart from the sheer military might and preparedness of the white Republic of South Africa, Rhodesia and the Portuguese authorities in Angola and Moçambique, reference has already been made to the point of view of responsible African leaders that the physical presence of the white man in Africa is not resented. In the words of Ndbaningi Sithole, African nationalism as expressed by the Bantu peoples does not hate the white man. His physical presence in Africa is welcome but his domination is unwelcome.

(Morphologically "domination" and "paternalism" mean more

or less the same thing – the Latin roots of the words, *dominus* and *pater* had very similar meanings in Roman society, but whereas paternalism in Southern Africa used to be accepted as a fairly harmonious situation, domination suggests conflict).

The problems of competitive nationalism among the numerically significant groups of people in Southern Africa consequently cannot be solved by removing either of its premises. It can only be solved by containing both elements in a constitutional framework which turns these elements into forces of value rather than forces of destruction.

In the history of economic thought formulae for such a constitutional exercise have received a great deal of attention and economics could, if given the opportunity, indicate the way out. The science has achieved some success in other fields on similar problems, such as the problems of destructive monopolies, "beggar my neighbour policies" in international trade, explosive farm price cycles, etc. In general, the basis of the solution is the definition of boundary conditions for the free play of individual action, and the special promotion through state aid of the backward but potentially viable infant.

In the present problem, a number of constitutional solutions have been offered by South Africans of various political convictions. We do not propose to survey these solutions in these pages. Our purpose was rather to investigate only one alternative, namely the proposition that the element of several different and numerically significant peoples plus the element of nationalism require the economic development of the several regions which the various peoples of the sub-continent regard as their homelands. The main practical target of this solution would be the creation of sufficient employment and income opportunities in these respective regions.

2. *The identification of the nations*
The geographical area involved in our discussion is roughly the sub-continent below the 6th-parallel, i.e. including Angola, Zambia, Malawi and Moçambique. (See Map No. 1). This area comprises approximately 2.3 million square miles. The whole area cannot, however, be regarded as suitable for the development of civilised communities, since large parts consist of desert and

14

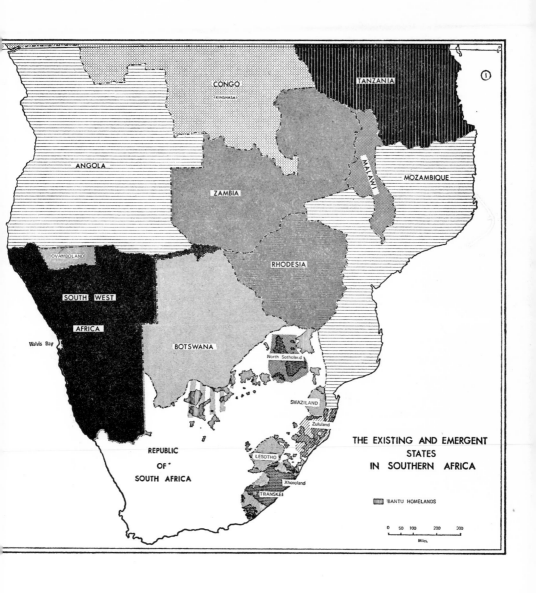

THE EXISTING AND EMERGENT
STATES
IN SOUTHERN AFRICA

‖‖‖‖ 'BANTU HOMELANDS

0   50 100   200   300
Miles.

semi-desert areas such as the Kalahari or swamps such as in the Okavango. The arid regions are usually traversed by nomadic peoples such as the Bushmen, who do live in closely-knit social patterns but of a very primitive nature, social patterns which do not by any stretch of imagination provide a basis for economic development in the sense usually understood. Apart from these tribes the land is used for extensive cattle farming by a small number of individual White or Bantu farmers. Consequently, it would be most misleading to regard the entire 2.3 million square miles as comparable to, say, the area of Europe or North America.

Within the bounds of this area a human population of approximately 45 million people is found, whose present geographic distribution over the sub-continent is explained partly by history and partly by geography.

The largest proportion of these peoples came to the sub-continent from the North during the sixteenth and seventeenth centuries. They are the Bantu peoples, a generic term used for the descendants of the Hamite peoples and the Negroes. They began to move into the sub-continent by the turn of the sixteenth century. As is well known the "White" South Africans descended from European stock who entered Southern Africa at the southernmost point of the Cape of Good Hope towards the middle of the seventeenth century. As their settlements gradually expanded towards the North-East, the Europeans by the turn of the eighteenth century came in contact with the southern moving Bantu tribes roughly between the Kei- and Keiskamma rivers. (The present area of the Ciskei near the port of East London).

These historical movements of population were determined both by the geographical possibilities of cattle raising and farming as well as political factors, such as the centrifugal forces of tribal wars among the Bantu further North and, as far as the White settlers were concerned, the extremely regimented policies of the Dutch East India Company and their successors, the British Colonial Office.

Geographically the land along the Eastern sea board from Cape Town in the South up to Beira in the North was at the time by far the most fertile of the entire sub-continent, in view of its greater rainfall.

Towards the end of the nineteenth century and particularly

during the first decade of the twentieth century the spread of the population began to be influenced very strongly by the geographical distribution of mineral wealth, in particular gold and diamonds. These and other minerals, such as copper, iron ore, manganese, platinum and chrome happened to occur in the interior regions, away from the traditional settlements of the greater part of the population. This explains very largely the changes in the internal migration of population since the beginning of this century when the exploitation of these mineral resources became economically attractive.

Finally, trading activities explain the early appearance of population concentrations in suitable harbour areas of Cape Town, Port Elizabeth, East London, Durban, Lourenço Marques and Beira.

Along the Western sea board, the nature of the coast forbade the development of natural harbours except at Swakopmund where a German harbour was established, and at Walvis Bay where the English shortly afterwards gained a foothold. At the same time the area had little economic attraction.

These were the historical, geographical and early economic determinants of the spread of the population over the sub-continent.

But, whatever geography dictated in this matter, it was clear from the start that among these peoples there existed divided political loyalties (based on tribal affiliation among the Bantu peoples, and historical connections with their European origins among the Whites). These different political loyalties and affinities could at the same time be related to broad social and cultural differences in ways of life and in general outlook as well as stages of development.

As early as the days of the London missionaries, and the English governors, Charles Somerset and George Grey, the areas now known as the Transkei and Ciskei, were recognised as the political homelands of the Xhosa peoples. Later, in the old Transvaal Republic, President Paul Kruger gave increased recognition to areas in the Eastern Transvaal as the homelands of the Northern Pedi under their chief Sekukuni, while Britain gave political recognition to the Matabele nation under their chief Lobengula. With the establishment of the Union of South Africa as a political entity in 1910 the British Government gave specific recognition to the politically separate interests of Bechuanaland (now Botswana), Basutoland (now Lesotho) and Swaziland, which became known as the "High Commission Territories".

North of the Limpopo River, up to the Zambesi and even further north, British influence developed under separate constitutions which later became the colonies of Southern Rhodesia (now Rhodesia), Northern Rhodesia (now Zambia) and Nyasaland (now Malawi). On the east and west sea boards Portuguese influence took the shape of two large provinces, namely Angola – a vast spreading land of low bush and high temperatures on the western side – and Moçambique – an elongated strip along the east coast running for about 1,400 miles from the South African province of Natal in the South, bordering Rhodesia and Malawi towards the interior and up to Tanzania in the North.

The area of South West Africa represents the only German historical interest in the sub-continent. German interest started in 1883 when the German merchant F. A. E. Lüderitz, purchased land – the Bay of Angra Pequena, and an adjacent strip of land along the coast – from a Nama chief. The outcome of his appeals for German protection was a German Protectorate proclaimed in 1884. Although German rule was firmly established between the years of 1907 and 1914, the entire area soon afterwards became a mandate of the South African Government in terms of the Treaty of Versailles. The current political position of South West Africa has recently been thoroughly examined by the World Court (in view of the disappearance of the League of Nations under which the Mandate was held) whose ultimate verdict amounted to a full recognition of the sovereignty of the South African Government.

Since the middle of the twentieth century most of these historically defined political boundaries came under scrutiny. New political constitutions developed rapidly, many of which have already received international recognition, such as the governments of Malawi, Zambia, Botswana, Lesotho and Swaziland. Others, such as the governments of the Transkei and Ovamboland are still in the process of formation. Some others, such as Rhodesia and perhaps the Portuguese areas, remain problematic.

Finally, there are the number of Bantu nations still within the constitution of the Republic whose political future is even more vague at this stage. Although still integral parts of the South African Republic, these Bantu nations have all received different degrees of authority and administrative powers of execution.

It would appear therefore that our sub-continent is in the process of a very extensive evolution, if not a peaceful revolution in its political structure. In the analysis we have in mind we have thought it advisable to cast our eyes on the possible future structure rather than to feel bound by the historical background. The following list of the separate political units or states is therefore put forward as a reasonable hypothesis upon which the political economy of Southern Africa may rest during the remainder of this century:

- the states that emerged from the decomposed Central African Federation, namely Malawi, Zambia and Rhodesia;
- the earstwhile "High Commission Territories" namely Botswana, Lesotho and Swaziland;
- the two Portuguese controlled provinces, Angola and Moçambique;
- the Bantu states emerging from the constitutional evolution taking place within the present Republic of South Africa. They are "Xhosaland", comprising the present constitutionally developed Transkei, and the Ciskei which has not yet developed politically to the same extent; "Zululand" in the Natal region, "North Sotholand" in the North Eastern Transvaal where the eventual integration of different ethnic groups such as the Pedi, who are the dominant people, the Shangaan, the Venda, Ndebele and the Swazi seems inevitable for practical reasons;
- the Republic of South Africa, excluding the abovementioned Bantu areas;
- Ovamboland in the North of South West Africa; and
- South West Africa, excluding Ovamboland.

The foregoing leaves unallocated, the approximately one million Tswana people who live on about four million morgen of land scattered over a wide area adjacent to Botswana and with regard to whom some territorial negotiations with the latter state may have to be considered by the Republic in future; and the approximately one million South Sotho people who culturally, and possibly even politically, belong to Lesotho. Within the borders of the Republic only Witzieshoek, a small area of 55,000 morgen, has been reserved for them, but as historians will confirm a much greater area within a ten mile strip east of the Caledon River and known as the "verowerde gebied" (conquered area), has often been claimed by Basuto leaders as belonging to them. In this respect, the late Dr. Verwoerd in a major policy speech in Pretoria on the 3rd September, 1963, as Prime Minister of the Republic, did advance some proposals. Dealing with the relationships between South Africa and the former "High Commission Territories" (Botswana, Lesotho and Swaziland), he said: "Close liaison with the territories would create new opportunities more quickly for those black areas at present under our control which are their neighbours and for which we are seeking further development and freedom. Were it possible for them to be joined to those 'High Commission Territories' to which their peoples are ethnically linked, then the present difficulty of establishing one big Tswana area or one large Sotho or Swazi area in Southern Africa, would fall away". Some days later he added: "Where desirable, the Republic would be prepared to help the Bantu of these territories to regain, by purchase or exchange, areas at present occupied by Whites", and that "the economic development of these territories could be planned and financed in co-ordination with that of the Republic, whose economy is of fundamental importance to them".

Finally, there is the remaining non-White population of South West Africa, who is not of Bantu origin but of a very heterogeneous ethnic nature, including Bushmen, Hottentot and Coloured blood. It must frankly be admitted, that their political future is highly problematic.

Equally problematic from a purely political point of view may be the so-called "Coloured population" who is concentrated in the Western and Eastern Cape Province and the Asiatic population, mainly concentrated in Natal. If we remind ourselves of the way in which we defined our problem in this work, namely that of the *economic* relationships between nations, as well as the given fact that thus far no serious proposal for a geographic area for these two groups of peoples has been put forward, it is clear that for economists, and for the discussion of economic relationships, these Coloured and Asiatic peoples have to be regarded as citizens of the Republic of South Africa.

Although it is usually assumed that by far the greatest proportion of a nation's peoples live within its boundaries, it is not necessarily the case in our "model". The lack of historical definition of geographical boundaries and political authority, the ease of migration, the absorbtive capacity of a few islands of economic activity in a sea of economic backwardness, the integrated nature of political authority under colonial and republican rule up to the present, all contributed to a state of affairs where the normal image of a nation as defined in the previous sentence, does not necessarily apply in Southern Africa.

In the description of the problem in hand it is consequently useful to distinguish between the so-called *de facto* populations, living in the territories or homelands, and the *de jure* populations, that is the total number of people belonging to a particular nation but living anywhere in the sub-continent. The problem could then be defined in terms of the differences between the *de facto* and *de jure* populations respectively of each homeland.

Table I contains estimates of the population sizes, the areas and the incomes of these separate nations. Some of the figures should of course be regarded as no more than rough indications of the orders of magnitude since the census data cannot be regarded as completely reliable; the incomes figures even less so. Moreover, substantial consolidation and exchange of territories may still have to come about, as was suggested above. Table II is so drawn up that the differences between the *de facto* and *de jure* populations of each territory can be clearly read off. Thus, for example, of the just over 3.2 million Zulu people only 1.3 million live in the approximately 12,000 square miles of their homeland. The balance was scattered all over the Republic of South Africa, from the surrounding Natal area where about 500,000 could be found down to the Cape Peninsula where about 2,000 were recorded in the 1960 census. About 371,000 lived in the Southern Transvaal where, in fact, they were the largest single ethnic group second only to the Whites.

A notable feature of Table II is the difference between the *de facto* and *de jure* population of the "Republic of South Africa"

TABLE I – THE AREA, POPULATION AND INCOME OF THE COUNTRIES IN SOUTHERN AFRICA, 1965

Country or nation	Area	Population		Product (income)	
		De facto	De jure	Gross domestic product	Income of de jure population
	Square miles	1,000	1,000	Rm	Rm
1. Angola	481,363	5,154	5,174	603	600
2. Botswana	219,921	559	619	28	41
Tswana areas in S.A. ...	12,679	439	1,218	16	129
3. Lesotho	11,716	841	1,038	33	77
South Sotho areas in S.A. ...	182	12	1,218	0.5	129
4. Malawi	46,067	4,042	4,265	116	174
5. Moçambique...	302,336	6,956	7,233	744	789
6. North Sotholand	14,475	872	2,089	27	199
7. Ovamboland	15,300	225	264	8	17
8. Republic of South Africa (excluding Bantu homelands)	413,989	13,285	5,797	7,175	5,854
9. Rhodesia	150,336	4,260	3,967	706	622
10. South West Africa (excluding Ovamboland) ...	302,967	373	336	204	154
11. Swaziland	6,704	379	418	60	55
Swazi areas in S.A.	600	50	336	2	32
12. Xhosaland	17,937	1,875	3,411	66	350
13. Zambia	290,592	3,712	3,766	546	505
14. Zululand	12,183	1,334	3,213	40	328
TOTAL	2,299,347	44,368	44,362	10,374	10,055

as we have defined it. Whereas about 13.3 million people are found physically within the boundaries of the Republic, only 5.8 million are regarded as *de jure* citizens of the Republic. This ratio does not, however, mean that the small number of Whites in the Republic are endeavouring to maintain an unjustifiable foothold on the country to the exclusion of others who may have greater claim to it. When these figures are broken down by region, it appears that in the Southern Transvaal, which has become the heartland of the Republic, the White population is the dominant group, numbering 1.1 million people, followed by the Zulus, numbering 371,000, the Tswanas, 263,000 and so on.

Differences between the *de facto* and *de jure* populations of any given territory in our list are not in themselves of any direct significance politically or culturally. The modern world is well acquainted with the fact that proportions of the populations of economically retarded areas have to seek employment beyond their borders to increase the national income. No one regards it as essential that *all* the members of a particular nation should be economically

(11)		(12)	(13)	(14)	(15)	(16)
...aziland	Swazi areas in S.A.	Xhosaland (Transkei and Ciskei)	Zambia	Zululand	Rest of the world	Total *de jure* population
—	—	—	1	—	—	5,174
—	—	—	—	—	—	619
—	—	—	—	—	—	1,218
—	—	—	—	—	—	1,038
—	—	—	—	—	—	1,218
—	—	—	6	—	4	4,625
—	—	—	1	—	15	7,233
—	—	—	—	—	—	2,089
—	—	—	—	—	—	264
—	—	—	—	—	—	5,797
—	—	—	6	—	—	3,967
—	—	—	—	—	—	336
379	—	—	—	—	—	418
—	50	—	—	—	—	336
—	—	1,875	—	—	—	3,411
—	—	—	3,695	—	5	3,766
—	—	—	—	1,334	—	3,213
—	—	—	3	—	—	30
379	50	1,875	3,712	1,334	24	44,392

	(4)	(5)	(6)	(7)	(8)	(9)	(10)	
uth tho as S.A.	Malawi	Moçam- bique	North Sotholand	Ovambo- land	Rep. of S.A. (excluding Bantu homelands)	Rhodesia	S.W.A. (excluding Ovambo- land)	S
—	—	—	—	—	11	8	—	
—	—	—	—	—	59	1	—	
—	—	—	—	—	779	—	—	
—	—	—	—	—	198	—	—	
2	—	—	—	—	1,206	—	—	
—	4,042	—	—	—	63	150	—	
—	—	6,956	—	—	161	100	—	
—	—	—	872	—	1,217	—	—	
—	—	—	—	225	—	—	39	
—	—	—	—	—	5,797	—	—	
—	—	—	—	—	18	3,943	—	
—	—	—	—	—	2	—	334	
—	—	—	—	—	39	—	—	
—	—	—	—	—	286	—	—	
—	—	—	—	—	1,536	—	—	
—	—	—	—	—	16	50	—	
—	—	—	—	—	1,879	—	—	
—	—	—	—	—	19	8	—	
2	4,042	6,956	872	225	13,285	4,260	373	

TABLE II – THE DE FACTO AND DE JURE POPULATI
IN SOUTHERN AFRICA,
(1,000)

De facto population \ De jure population	(1) Angola	(2) Botswana	Tswana areas in S.A.	(3) Lesotho	ii
1. Angola	5,154	—	—	—	
2. ⎰ Botswana ...	—	559	—	—	
Tswana areas in S.A. ...	—	—	439	—	
3. ⎰ Lesotho ...	—	—	—	841	
South Sotho areas in S.A. ...	—	—	—	—	
4. Malawi	—	—	—	—	
5. Moçambique ...	—	—	—	—	
6. North Sotholand	—	—	—	—	
7. Ovamboland ...	—	—	—	—	
8. Republic of S.A. (Excluding Bantu homelands) ...	—	—	—	—	
9. Rhodesia ...	—	—	—	—	
10. S.W.A. (Excluding Ovamboland) ...	—	—	—	—	
11. ⎰ Swaziland ...	—	—	—	—	
Swazi areas ...					
in S.A. ...	—	—	—	—	
12. Xhosaland (Transkei and Ciskei)	—	—	—	—	
13. Zambia	—	—	—	—	
14. Zululand ...	—	—	—	—	
15. Rest of the World	—	—	—	—	
16. Total de facto pop.	5,154	559	439	841	

active *within* the political boundaries. Problems only begin to arise if this tendency proceeds so far that the homeland of the worker becomes nothing but an economically sterile reservation or in other words a dormant dormatory. At that stage the realism of the political image of the separate nations also becomes problematic. It may perhaps be threatening many of the areas identified in Table I. If the ratio between the *de facto* and *de jure* populations is defined as the "absence co-efficient", it will be found that for many of these territories this co-efficient is extremely high.

To make matters worse, the absence from the homelands is very largely concentrated among the male population between the ages of 20 to 45 years, the latter being the age of retirement for many Bantu in their traditional societies.

In the case of the Bantu peoples of South Africa, the majority of the economically active Bantu males are either temporarily or permanently active *outside* the borders of their homelands. For example, of the 422,000 economically active Xhosa males of the Transkei, 193,000 (roughly 45 per cent) were thus absent in 1960. It seems probable that the total addition to the economically active male population of the Transkei seeks employment outside the territory. In this respect, the other Bantu homelands may be in a similar or a worse predicament. To these figures should of course be added the new entrants to the labour market from the growth of the Bantu populations *de facto* permanently established outside the borders of the homelands.

It should be clear to any realistic observer that there can be no possibility of creating employment opportunities in the retarded or backward areas of Southern Africa to the extent of absorbing, not only the growth of the *de facto* population but also the accretion to the *de jure* population as well as the existing number of people outside the borders of these territories. More realistic targets would have to be envisaged which would offer an answer to the problem of political nationalism on the one hand, and, on the other hand, be economically feasible. This means that, however rapidly the retarded areas are developed over the next few decades, there will always remain a significant absence co-efficient – a number of people *temporarily* absent from their homelands. This still remains a vast proposition for it seems that according to the census figures 53.5 per cent of the *de jure* population of the Bantu homelands in South Africa can be regarded as continuously absent from the areas, while 6.2 per cent may be regarded as temporarily absent.

The position with regard to the various Bantu nations in the Republic of South Africa is illustrated in Table III. This table shows the percentage of Bantu males between the ages of 15 and 64 (a) continuously absent from their homelands, and (b) temporarily absent from their homelands. (The Bantu from states outside the borders of the Republic are all regarded as temporarily present in the Republic).

Our point of view that economic co-operation among the nations of Southern Africa need not exclude the use of temporary workers in the Republic from other states, does not imply that the present *continuously* absent population of approximately 6 million (related to the adult Bantu male population of 1.3 million) has been or could be transferred to their homelands within the foreseeable future. Neither does it mean that the *temporarily* absent population of about 650,000 should not be increased in future. What could be realistically aimed at is a reduction of the 6 million and an increase in the 650,000 in such a way that the absence co-efficient of each homeland is reduced significantly.

In fact, from a qualitative point of view the dynamism of the social structure in the homelands would be very substantially served by the return of a percentage of the continuously absent population from, for instance, sophisticated urban Bantu residential areas like Soweto, Mamelodi, Langa, etc. In view of the acculturation to which they have been subjected in these cities, their improved economic motivation, their higher economic abilities and more rational principles of economic behaviour, these families would be a tremendous stimulant to the communities in the various homelands. They would, for one thing, be far less sensitive to local taboos and other restrictions on economic enterprise and modern ways of living. In other words, the development of these homelands would be best served by a two-way migration during the next few decades. A return flow of families at present considered to be *continuously* absent from their homelands in the "white cities", and an outward flow of young men from their homelands seeking temporary work and training in the "white cities". Such a situation would contribute much to the economic

TABLE III – THE ABSENCE OF BANTU MALES FROM THEIR HOMELANDS, 1960

Bantu nation	Male absence co-efficients[1]				Percentage of population			
	1936	1946	1951	1960	In homeland	Temporarily absent	Continuously absent	Total
Ciskei Xhosa ...	27.5	24.9	24.1	23.4	49.1	14.9	36.0	100.0
Transkei Xhosa ...	23.1	24.3	25.4	25.1	47.7	16.0	36.3	100.0
Zulu	23.4	27.6	29.8	25.8	36.0	12.4	51.6	100.0
Tswana	28.2	24.5	23.9	20.6	33.7	8.8	57.5	100.0
North-Sotho... ...								
Shangaan/Tsonga ...								
Swazi...	21.8	27.9	32.4	28.6	31.9	12.9	55.2	100.0
Ndebele								
Venda								
South-Sotho	33.7	30.0	27.3	19.2	0.9	0.2	98.9	100.0

1) *Males temporarily absent expressed as a percentage of the sum of males continuously present and temporarily absent.*

improvement of the social framework in these homelands as discussed in Chapter IV.

According to the census data, the entrepreneurial and enterprise talent among the Bantu are concentrated outside these areas, mostly in the abovementioned residential areas near the metropolitan cities, while the populations in the reserves consist mainly of completely unskilled, untrained, mostly fairly lethargic Bantu. Very little could accordingly be achieved in the Bantu homelands by merely mobilising the present manpower position. In order to employ more of the unskilled Bantu it would be necessary to complement them with a greater number of experienced and motivated members of their community.

For this reason, calculations of the desired number of employment opportunities to be created in the various homelands, should not be cast in superficial statistical terms. Although such calculations are useful in order to obtain some idea of the order of magnitude, the process of creating such employment opportunities should be viewed in the light of the above argument.

CHAPTER II

THE ECONOMICS OF THE PROBLEM

1. *Introduction*

It has been made clear in the previous chapter that our problem mainly boils down to the creation of employment opportunities in the various homelands or states of the several nations at present living in the sub-continent of Africa.

The creation of these employment opportunities could in principle be approached from several ideological points of view. Economic history has provided us with at least three main lines of thought, namely that of (i) *laissez faire*, (ii) the communistic approach of central planning and balanced growth, and (iii) the method of systematic co-operation between politically independent or fairly independent and responsible states, based on the economic principle of *comparative* advantage of production in the various regions. Put in a somewhat different way, *laissez faire* would be equivalent to the political pattern of integration. The communistic approach as applied by Russia over the last two decades leads very largely to economic and political isolation from the rest of the world and a completely independent pace and pattern of growth. The third alternative, which we defined as "systematic co-operation" between politically independent states, is the subject of this chapter.

As will become clear in the following pages the economic principle upon which systematic co-operation between politically independent states rests, is the well-known theory of *comparative advantage* in production-opportunities.

According to this theory an area which superficially possesses no *absolute* cost advantages of production need not lose its entire economically active population through emigration. As long as some production possibilities exist the area will have *comparative* advantages in certain directions, *viz-a-viz* other areas. The problem of policy is to convert these comparative cost advantages into absolute price advantages, particularly in respect of those industries with an export potential.

The limit below which this principle would have no practical application is set by the per capita income which could be generated along these lines. In general, comparative cost advantages are translated into price advantages and export potential through a lowering of wage levels, devaluation or subsidisation.

These policy measures, in fact, mean that the community has to set its national income per capita at a level which makes an export trade in goods and services rather than an emigration of labour possible. A critical choice between trade and emigration thus arises if the national income level required for trade, rather than emigration, falls below some minimum subsistence level.

In the communist system of economic planning as developed in the Soviet, the principle of comparative advantage has been completely overlooked, probably due to the size and resource diversity of the Soviet Union making international trade relatively unimportant for the achievement of its goals.

In the satellite countries which adopted the Russian methods of planning, this approach soon ran into serious difficulties because of its inability to consider the advantages these satellites could secure from trade.

In the sub-continent of Africa it may be expected that this approach would run into similar difficulties. Their modest size, the low level of development and diversification, the lack of diversified resources and the historical links with the economy of the Republic would seem to rule out this possibility completely. Their obvious procedure is consequently that of the principle of comparative advantage. In this respect the traditional objections against the principle, namely, that it is too static and does not take into account the broader macro-economic possibilities, have to a very large extent been removed by recent research and practical applications such as in the programmes in Puerto Rico, the Philippines, and Israel.

The application of the principle of comparative advantage was perhaps obvious in view of the geographic situation of these three countries. The Philippines and Puerto Rico are both islands, while Israel could, in a political sense, be regarded as an island in the midst of Arab hostility, seeking its economic relationships further afield. In the South African case the contiguity of these areas to each other and the already mentioned ease of migration, have perhaps blurred our ability to envisage the applicability

(11)		(12)	(13)	(14)	(15)	(16)
‚vaziland	Swazi areas in S.A.	Xhosaland (Transkei areas Ciskei)	Zambia	Zululand	Rest of the World	Total income of *de jure* population
—	—	—	1	—	—	600
—	—	—	—	—	—	41
—	—	—	—	—	—	129
—	—	—	—	—	—	77
—	—	—	—	—	—	129
—	—	—	6	—	—	174
—	—	—	—	—	—	789
—	—	—	—	—	—	199
—	—	—	—	—	—	17
3	—	13	10	3	28	5,854
—	—	—	10	—	3	622
—	—	—	—	—	—	154
50	—	—	—	—	—	55
—	2	—	—	—	—	32
—	—	53	—	—	—	350
—	—	—	472	—	15	505
—	—	—	—	37	—	328
7	—	—	47	—	—	365
60	2	66	546	40	46	10,420

	(4)	(5)	(6)	(7)	(8)	(9)	(10)	
outh otho reas S.A.	Malawi	Moçam-bique	North Sotholand	Ovambo-land	Rep. of S.A. (excluding Bantu homelands)	Rhodesia	S.W.A. (excluding Ovambo-land)	S
—	—	—	—	—	3	—	—	
—	—	—	—	—	14	—	—	
—	—	—	—	—	117	—	—	
—	—	—	—	—	44	—	—	
).5	—	—	—	—	129	—	—	
—	112	—	—	—	20	36	—	
—	—	734	—	—	40	15	—	
—	—	—	23	—	176	—	—	
—	—	—	—	7	—	—	10	
—	—	1	4	1	5,733	28	25	
—	—	1	—	—	16	592	—	
—	—	—	—	—	3	—	151	
—	—	—	—	—	5	—	—	
—	—	—	—	—	30	—	—	
—	—	—	—	—	297	—	—	
—	—	—	—	—	5	13	—	
—	—	—	—	—	291	—	—	
—	4	8	—	—	252	22	18	
).5	116	744	27	8	7,175	706	204	

TABLE IV – THE GROSS DOMESTIC PRODUCT AND N
(NATIONAL UNITS) IN SOUTHER
(R millions)

Income of nations	(1)	(2)		(3)	
Gross domestic product (GDP.)	Angola	Botswana	Tswana areas in S.A.	Lesotho	S S a in
1. Angola	596	—	—	—	
2. { Botswana ...	—	27	—	—	
Tswana areas in S.A. ...	—	—	12	—	
3. { Lesotho ...	—	—	—	33	
South Sotho areas in S.A. ...	—	—	—	—	
4. Malawi	—	—	—	—	
5. Moçambique ...	—	—	—	—	
6. North Sotholand	—	—	—	—	
7. Ovamboland ...	—	—	—	—	
8. Republic of S.A. (Excluding Bantu homelands) ...	—	1	4	—	
9. Rhodesia ...	—	—	—	—	
10. S.W.A. (Excluding Ovamboland) ...	—	—	—	—	
11. { Swaziland ...	—	—	—	—	
Swazi areas in S.A. ...	—	—	—	—	
12. Xhosaland (Transkei and Ciskei)	—	—	—	—	
13. Zambia	—	—	—	—	
14. Zululand ...	—	—	—	—	
15. Rest of the World	7	—	—	—	
16. Total GDP. ...	603	28	16	33	

of the principle of comparative advantage. As the political definition becomes clearer we believe this principle would also increasingly assert itself.

2. *Patterns of production and trade in the sub-continent*

In order to draw the broadest outline of the economic dimensions of our problem, we shall have to distinguish between the gross domestic product of each area, on the one hand, and the total national income of each community, on the other hand, which in practice means the total income of the *de jure* population of each area, earned anywhere within or outside the area. In any normally viable economy differences between these two concepts should not be very large, in the same sense as in the previous chapter the differences between the *de facto* and *de jure* populations of any area should not be very large.

The fact is, however, as is depicted in Table IV that of an output of almost R10,000 million produced in the sub-continent, more than 74 per cent originated within the borders of the Republic and only 26 per cent in the other states. Of this amount almost 40 per cent was earned by the peoples of these states while 62 per cent accrued to the citizens of the Republic. The most casual inspection of Table IV would reveal the extent to which each nation is dependent for its income on the productive processes within the borders of the Republic of South Africa rather than on its own resources and economic system.

From the information contained in Chapter I it is clear that the only three states whose *de facto* populations exceeded the *de jure* populations by substantial margins were South West Africa, Rhodesia, and the Republic of South Africa. The situations in these countries, where the availability of natural resources, entrepreneurship and the availability of skills to complement the employment of unskilled labour, are such that the employment possibilities greatly exceed the available local unskilled labour supplies.

A closer inspection of the population figures in Table I and the income figures in Table IV reveals a fairly high correlation between the per capita products of the states and the percentage of income of the *de jure* population earned in the countries themselves. Thus, South West Africa, with a product per capita of

R547 generated 98 per cent of its *de jure* population's income itself. Next in rank was the Republic of South Africa with a per capita product of R540 and a locally generated income of 96 per cent, followed by Rhodesia with a per capita product of R166 and a locally generated income of 95 per cent, Zambia, R147 and 93 per cent and so downwards towards Xhosaland with a product per capita of R35 and a locally generated income of 15 per cent, followed by Zululand and North Sotholand, each with a product per capita of approximately R30 and a locally generated income of 12 per cent.

With due regard to the fact that these kinds of national income estimates may include several marginal incomparabilities, it would nevertheless appear that the only area significantly deviating from the correlation may be Angola with a domestic product per capita of approximately R117 and a percentage of locally generated income of 99. It is possible that Malawi, with a product per capita of approximately R29 and a percentage of locally generated income of approximately 65 may be in the same position although here the method of calculation of the national income may disturb the pattern substantially. However, in those cases the explanation of the deviation may be found in the fact that these states are institutionally and geographically fairly far removed from the metropolitan areas of employment so that the lack of mobility may partly be explained by ignorance of the possibilities of increasing the income by migration.

That the product per capita figures obtained under present circumstances need not necessarily correctly reflect the employment potential of various areas, may be suggested by a comparison between the position of the Swazi areas in the Republic compared with that of Swaziland itself, as well as the comparison between the position of the Tswana areas within the Republic and that of Botswana. In both cases the South African areas showed much smaller products per capita as well as lower locally generated income percentages. Although, we hesitate to draw this conclusion firmly, it would appear on the surface as if the Republican areas up to the present, have been used as reservoirs of labour, while in the already politically less dependent states of the same ethnic groups, better efforts had apparently been made to create local employment opportunities. At the same time, the influx control of the Republic may have discriminated in favour of the local areas as against migration from the politically less dependent states. This point is further illustrated by the fact that the average income earned by Bantu in all industrial sectors within the Republic vary between R250 and R280 per annum.

The present distribution of the gross domestic products of the various states and homelands and the distribution of the economically active population indicate very clearly that the local pattern of production at present offers little scope for economic growth. In most cases the population is concentrated either on agricultural, forestry, hunting, or mining activities. Mining activities occur predominantly in Zambia (38 per cent of the gross domestic product) South West Africa (47 per cent of the gross domestic product) Swaziland (14 per cent of the gross domestic product). A typical case of agricultural domination is the Transkei where 222,000 or 93 per cent of the 243,000 men who were economically active in 1960, were engaged in agriculture, about 10,000 or 4 per cent in services while the remaining 3 per cent were spread among four sectors – mining, manufacturing, construction and trade.

According to national accounts figures, considerable construction activity was registered in Swaziland in 1964 (26 per cent of the gross domestic product) and Lesotho (24 per cent of the gross domestic product in 1965/66). Construction should be regarded as a highly fluctuating aspect of economic activity in these areas and may not represent the same high percentage of local production each year. Thus in the case of Swaziland, for example, the high figure is explained by the building of the railway line from the iron ore fields to the eastern sea board in Moçambique. In Lesotho the improvement of the road system explains the largest part of construction activities in that area. If, as in the case of South Africa, a sustained process of growth can be generated, employment in construction should become a permanent feature of the gross national products of these countries.

The main reason why any projected pattern of employment in these areas cannot be based on the present industrial distribution and concentration on agriculture, is to be found in the fact that agricultural production is organised on subsistence lines and that the farming units are too small. It was established by the Tomlinson

31

Commission[1] and others that agriculture could not provide more than about half of the present population of the South African Bantu homelands with a means of livelihood. The correct managerial optimum, in terms of size of land per person, would render many of the present "active population" superfluous. This would mean, paradoxically, that in order to exploit the most important economic asset of these areas, namely land, the employment problem in these areas would be aggravated.

The foregoing does not imply that the development of agriculture should not receive high priority. On the contrary, some of the most important immediate steps to be taken would lie in this field. It is quite probable that agricultural developments will bring about the greatest immediate increases in the gross domestic product. The increased incomes from agricultural expansion, might, however, provide some excess resources with which employment opportunities could be created elsewhere. Neither does the foregoing mean that the surplus population displaced from agriculture, could be indiscriminately employed in industry. Since the "skill mix" in industrial activity would require, as we have argued before, the return to these areas of fairly sophisticated Bantu from the present metropolitan areas in the Republic, a high percentage of the displaced agricultural workers would in the meantime have to find their way towards temporary unskilled employment in the Republic.

In whatever way the problem of employment is tackled, the conclusion that these areas would have to industrialize, seems inescapable. Equally inescapable is the conclusion that industrial activities cannot be based on the respective local markets. Any significant industrial activity would have to be orientated towards "export markets" until local incomes have increased sufficiently to provide a domestic market. (Since these areas do already import substantial quantities of industrial goods, some possibilities may exist for import replacement of such goods. Import replacement, however, requires a domestic market at least large enough to sustain a reasonably productive capacity as compared to the cost at which foreign supplies provide such goods.)

Since all the underdeveloped areas involved have been, until

1. *Report of the Commission for the Socio-economic development of the Bantu areas in the Union of South Africa*, Government Printer, Pretoria, 1955.

(11)		(12)	(13)	(14)	(15)	(16)
‥waziland	Swazi areas in S.A.	Xhosaland (Transkei and Ciskei)	Zambia	Zululand	Rest of the World	Total Exports
—	—	—	259	—	154,613	158,436
—	—	—	311	—	4,600	9,281
—	—	—	—	—	—	4,300
—	—	—	—	—	257	5,200
—	—	—	—	—	—	10
9	—	—	915	—	18,140	24,142
150	—	—	52	—	69,197	82,161
—	—	—	—	—	—	4,500
—	—	—	—	—	—	2,000
15,770	1,000	44,000	32,312	12,000	863,036	1,211,615
96	—	—	81,465	—	169,366	294,218
—	—	—	43	—	74,265	161,512
X	—	—	95	—	14,243	22,690
—	X	—	—	—	—	50
—	—	X	—	—	—	3,500
4	—	—	X	—	317,174	349,418
—	—	—	—	X	—	3,000
2,971	—	—	42,586	—	X	1,956,303
19,000	1,000	44,000	158,038	12,000	1,684,891	4,292,336

outh otho reas S.A.	(4) Malawi	(5) Moçambique	(6) North Sotholand	(7) Ovamboland	(8) Rep. of S.A. (excluding Bantu homelands)	(9) Rhodesia	(10) S.W.A. (excluding Ovamboland)	
—	7	2,137	—	—	1,308	112	—	
—	—	—	—	—	3,712	658	—	
—	—	—	—	—	4,300	—	—	
—	—	—	—	—	4,940	3	—	
X	—	—	—	—	10	—	—	
—	X	248	—	—	1,561	3,252	1	
—	460	X	—	—	7,083	2,754	—	
—	—	—	X	—	4,500	—	—	
—	—	—	—	X	1,000	—	—	
200	1,089	18,286	10,000	2,000	X	59,894	124,000	
—	14,459	2,335	—	—	21,955	X	120	
—	—	—	—	1,000	86,902	112	X	
—	—	74	—	—	8,148	130	—	
—	—	—	—	—	50	—	—	
—	—	—	—	—	3,500	—	—	
—	972	62	—	—	20,263	10,793	34	
—	—	—	—	—	3,000	—	—	
—	11,477	98,115	—	—	1,519,167	143,672	13,845	
200	28,464	121,257	10,000	3,000	1,690,589	221,390	139,000	

TABLE V – MERCHANDISE IMPORTS AND EXPORTS[1] OF SOUTHERN AFRICA, 1964
(R 1,000)

EXPORTS IMPORTS	(1) Angola	(2)	Tswana areas in S.A.	(3) Lesotho	
		Botswana	Tswana areas in S.A.	Lesotho	
1. Angola	X	—	—	—	
2. { Botswana ...	—	X	—	—	
Tswana areas in S.A. ...	—	—	X	—	
3. { Lesotho ...	—	—	—	X	
South Sotho areas in S.A. ...	—	—	—	—	
4. Malawi	—	6	—	—	
5. Moçambique ...	2,465	—	—	—	
6. North Sotholand	—	—	—	—	
7. Ovamboland ...	—	—	—	—	
8. Republic of S.A. (Excluding Bantu homelands) ...	2,153	4,665	6,000	15,210	
9. Rhodesia ...	451	3,964	—	7	
10. S.W.A. (Excluding Ovamboland ...	—	—	—	—	
11. { Swaziland ...	—	—	—	—	
Swazi areas in S.A. ...	—	—	—	—	
12. Xhosaland (Transkei and Ciskei)	—	—	—	—	
13. Zambia	14	102	—	—	
14. Zululand ...	—	—	—	—	
15. Rest of the World	122,195	592	—	1,683	
16. Total Imports ...	127,278	9,329	6,000	16.900	

1) Excluding gold and including re-exports.

recently, a part of a customs union with a much more developed area without much, if any, specific protection or subsidisation, their export trade was determined through the market mechanism by absolute cost advantages of which these areas had very little. The only possibility of greater trading activity would be through policy intervention by all the governments concerned acting in co-ordination with each other. Such an approach would only be feasible if a significantly large proportion of trade happens to be among the territories participating in the policy co-ordination on a sub-continental basis.

The present situation in this regard is described in a trade grid prepared from available official data and some unofficial estimates. The grid is set out in Table V under similar country headings as has been done with regard to Tables II and IV.

The most optimistic interpretation of the contents of Table V would be that the potential expansion of economic activity among the territories seems much greater than the existing orders of magnitude. The trade among the areas, excluding the Republic of South Africa and the rest of the world, amounts to only R130 million. This is only 11.6 per cent of the total exports of these areas to all countries and 14.2 per cent of their total imports from all countries. When the Republic of South Africa is added to the trade grid the position improves substantially, but the dependence on external trade relations remains very great. The total value of trade within this extended grid, including the Republic, amounts to R651 million. This amounts to 27.9 per cent of the total exports of the sub-continent to all countries and 25.0 per cent of total imports of the sub-continent from all countries. It may well be asked whether these percentages provide a realistic basis for planning of the kind we have in mind. Let us examine the cases in particular.

In the cases of Malawi, Zambia, Botswana, Lesotho, Swaziland and South West Africa the dependence upon imports from other parts of the sub-region is large, and in the case of Rhodesia, Botswana, Lesotho, Swaziland and South West Africa the dependence upon export markets within the sub-region is equally large. Angola and Moçambique trade fairly substantially with each other, but the bulk of their trade is with the rest of the world outside the sub-region.

The trading position of the Republic of South Africa at present completely dominates the character of the sub-regional grid; its trade representing more than 80 per cent of the total. At present, the Republic is very "outward orientated" in the sense that its trade with the rest of the world is roughly six times as large as its trade within the sub-region. Nevertheless, of the R651 million inter-territorial trade within the sub-regions, trade with the Republic accounts for 80 per cent. With regard to non-labour services, a somewhat similar pattern emerges from the available figures. The pattern with regard to labour services, has already been discussed.

A more optimistic view of this structural pattern of trade would be to recognise a basic complimentarity in the Republican trade with the sub-continent, on the one hand, and its trade mainly with Europe, on the other hand. To a large extent the Republic's economic ability to sustain a programme of political and economic viability for the new nations of this sub-continent, depends heavily on the continuation of its trade and financial relations with Europe.

The figures in table V emphasise the economic transformation that might be brought about in the sub-region with the co-operation of the Republic of South Africa. Simplifying somewhat: the present inter-regional pattern of activity is one of exchanging *labour* for *goods* which the Republic largely imports from the rest of the world. The desirable pattern, however, is a greater inter-regional flow of *goods*, at the expense of *labour migration* (subject to the qualifications already discussed), and trade with the rest of the world. In short, without necessarily reducing the R3,641 million trade with the rest of the world, the *percentage* dependence on the rest of the world could be reduced by rapidly increasing the inter-regional trade at present valued at about R651 million. *This would be the target.*

3. *The theoretical basis of systematic co-operation in the sub-continent*
At first sight it would seem that the achievement of the target mentioned above is extremely idealistic, especially in view of the fact that three-quarters of the existing trade of the sub-continent is with trading partners outside the group. On the other hand, it is quite true that this large gap is an indication of the potential

growth of inter-regional trade through the diversion of the extra-regional movement of goods and services. It is, however, hardly likely that this diversion of trade towards the members of the group will come about within the institutional arrangement of a so-called "common market" on lines similar to that of the European Economic Community. In the theory of customs unions, as developed since the writings of Jacob Viner, and even earlier those of Friedrich List, it has been recognised that a customs union is economically justified among states whose productive patterns are fairly competitive before union and which have the possibilities of becoming more complementary after union. Moreover, as was pointed out by List more than a hundred years ago, a pre-condition to success is that most members of the union should be at roughly the same level of economic development. Neither of these crucial preconditions exist in our case. Indeed, almost exactly the reverse applies. Not only are there great differences between the levels of economic development of the Republic of South Africa, Rhodesia, Malawi, etc., but the economies outside that of Rhodesia and the Republic at present show very little industrial or economic diversification and practically no competitiveness with that of the Republic.

It is also increasingly realised by economists such as Lionel Robbins, and by statesmen such as Walter Hallstein that a truly common market or economic community involves a large degree of political integration as well. This consideration alone rules out the possibility of a true customs union.

To our mind, the idea of a customs union points in the wrong direction. What is needed is more diversification and the development of greater competitiveness in the various member states. This would, by the same token, require the opposite of a common market and actually a certain protection of the industrial possibilities of the various regions. The protection would, however, have to take place within a broad overall plan for the sub-region as a whole, with the very positive co-operation of the Republic of South Africa.

The systematic co-operation proposed in this work would accordingly have to be planned on the basis of the inter-industrial relationships already existing in the sub-continent. At the moment these inter-relationships exist mainly in the input-output grid of the Republic. It would be economically very costly for the Republic to interfere seriously with the costs and prices of industries whose output of final goods or inputs of raw materials depend largely on markets and sources outside the sub-continent. It therefore seems practical to start with the broad proposition that those industries with high "inverse co-efficients" (that is those with several forward and backward linkages with other industries also operating in the grid) would be more amenable to positive planning than industries whose viability depends largely on export markets on the one hand or on the acquisition of raw materials and capital goods from abroad. One sector largely excluded from this exercise would be mining and certain types of agriculture such as sugar plantations, tobacco, tropical fruit etc., which require specific climatic conditions.

The principle of comparative advantage as a basis of planning the co-operation envisaged, would then be confined to more or less "foot loose" industries.

Judging by some calculations of forward and backward linkages made by Professor D. C. Krogh some years ago, the most interesting industrial sectors would be textiles, chemicals and iron and steel products and non-ferrous metal production. In all these cases both the forward and backward linkages with other industries existing in the sub-continent were high (65 per cent and upwards) which means that their economic viability depends very largely on economic conditions within the sub-continent. Moreover, none of these industries directly serve consumer demand, so that some of the immediate disadvantages of decentralised location could be absorbed within the rest of the industrial processes. In other cases such as processed food, grain mill products and leather products the backward linkages were large while, on the other hand, the dependence on final consumer demand was also high. This would, however, merely mean that increases in cost due to decentralised location, would have a direct bearing on the retail price level and could be offset in the planning process. In short, it would seem that priority might, from the point of view of plan-sensitivity be given to the so-called intermediate manufacturing processes and only in the second place to the so-called final manufacturing processes. This would, however, not be a hard and fast rule.

The application of the principle of comparative advantage to the planning of economic growth in undeveloped countries, is not as clear-cut as in the case of trade among industrially advanced countries. When the requirements of growth theory are taken into account, the simplicity, but not the logic of the classical principle breaks down, and would according to Professor H. B. Chenery,[1] place a greater reliance on general knowledge and intuition. This, Chenery feels, may be a practical advantage.

The most serious theoretical qualifications to the principle of comparative advantage come from the type of non-quantitative inter-dependence among sectors that is described by Professor A. O. Hirschmann. If as he supposes, one growth sequence is more effective than another in the sense that it economises on decision making ability or provides a greater incentive to political action, a set of criteria ostensibly having little to do with comparative advantage is implied. This qualification, however, merely serves to emphasise the fact that planning decisions are *in the last analysis* fairly subjective and based on the personal experience of the planner, since all these aspects lead to a conflict that cannot be resolved in economic terms.

Within the framework of the inter-industry grid of the Republic of South Africa the following steps seem to present a practical programme:

1) a broad reconnaissance of the various industries to exclude those that are clearly unsuitable for development in the under-developed areas and to identify those that would warrant further investigation; and

2) a more thorough study of the "possibles" with special reference to the following aspects:

   a) the employment co-efficient, that is the amount of employment which would result from the establishment of the particular factory itself, plus those that would result from the so-called linkage effects;

   b) the cost components which would indicate the relative comparative advantage (or comparative disadvantage) of location in the under-developed areas in comparison with location in the metropolitan areas of the Republic.

1. Chenery, H. B., "Comparative Advantage and Development Policy" in *Surveys of Economic Theory – Growth and Development*, Volume II, 1966, p. 129.

The most practical way of doing this, would be to obtain the cost breakdown of factories already situated in the metropolitan areas, and to determine the increases that would result from setting up similar processes in the under-developed areas by a process of inspection;

c) the demand aspect, that is, some idea of the elasticity of demand for the particular product in order to determine possibilities of expansion without having to consider important decreases in price and marginal revenue;

d) the capital component. As far as the typical comparative cost influence of high capital co-efficients are concerned, these would already have been studied under point (b) above, but apart from the cost aspect, the availability of capital also has to be considered as an independent factor;

e) the linkage effect, which has already been taken into account in calculating the direct and indirect employment effects. Further attention would also have to be paid to the possibility of certain types of industrial activities which could serve as general growth points around which various types of other economic activities could originate;

f) the so-called "marginal reinvestment criteria" which, according to many economists such as Professor W. Galenson, H. Leibenstein and H. B. Chenery would in under-developed countries also be necessary to take account of the division of income resulting from a project between profit and wages, since savings from the former are higher. The International Bank for Reconstruction and Development in its operations takes into account a similar norm, namely that of self-liquidation, in which preference is given to such enterprises which could repay loans out of their own earnings rather than from taxing the indirect beneficiaries from the project. The Galenson and Leibenstein variation would identify the most profitable project as the one with the highest capital labour ratio. This unfortunately leads to the rather paradoxical conclusion that the factor intensity rule followed under (b) and (d) above, should be reversed. Countries should prefer the most capital intensive rather than the least capital intensive techniques in order to promote saving and future growth. This is, however, merely another example of the fact that not all the criteria to be used in our program lead to exactly the same results and that in the final analysis some "subjective" valuation of the industrial priorities would have to be made by the planners themselves; and

g) finally, the so-called "non-quantitative inter-dependence among sectors", assumed by Professor Hirschman would have to be taken into account. According to Hirschman one growth sequence may be more effective than another because it economises on decision making ability or provides a greater incentive to political action. The relevance of this point to some of the under-developed areas in our model would seem to be obvious. This point is, however, fully discussed in Chapter IV below.

By means of these steps, we believe, it should be possible to decide on those industries which could most economically be established in the under-developed areas such as Swaziland, the Transkei, Malawi, etc. Since we have already indicated that this diffusion of location will not come about on the basis of the free market mechanism of essentially private decisions, the final step in the processing of the program would have to be a decision about the instruments to be applied by the planners in order to make the plan work despite the dictates of the free market mechanism.

4. *The policy instruments of co-operation*

Before proceeding, and in order to fix ideas, let us consider the fact that should these various members of the model have been politically independent to the extent that, not only labour migration was rigidly controlled but that they could also set their internal cost levels wherever they chose by means of exchange rate levels, much of our solution would depend on this instrument. As it is, the area is at present a full monetary union with the exception of Angola, Moçambique, Malawi, Zambia and Rhodesia. The Rhodesian monetary link with the Republic is becoming stronger, but in the other cases this is not so, as was illustrated by the devaluation of the Malawi pound in sympathy with sterling in November 1967. We shall have to return to the monetary aspect of our problem later on, but at this stage the fact that exchange rates as an instrument of economic co-operation in Southern Africa seems to provide very little scope, has to be recognised.

Economists are, however, well aware of the fact that a devaluation of currency could be simulated by a process of tariff protection-cum-export-subsidisation so that recourse may have to be had to these instruments.

As far as protection is concerned, this is already applied by Angola, Moçambique, Zambia, Malawi and Rhodesia, but these are at the same time the communities with the highest domestic products of the under-developed areas in our model. In comparison with the other areas, the already protected communities at least have the domestic market which is an essential pre-condition to the efficacy of import protection. For the Transkei, Swaziland, Lesotho etc., there would be practically no advantage at all in protecting their "domestic market" against competition from abroad. For the time being, industries to be established in these areas would have to depend for their turnover on sales outside the areas. They are consequently faced with the fact that full reliance would have to be placed on the instrument of export subsidies.

The final stage in the programming of economic operations, would therefore be to design *a policy of subsidisation* linked up with the investment priorities determined according to the principles suggested in section 3 above. Even in those areas where protection has become feasible, the instrument of subsidies may provide added advantages. Economists (e.g. Professor J. Tinbergen) have often claimed superiority for this alternative method of industrial stimulation.

The above suggestion would involve the planners in a full scale consideration of the method of financing the plan. The sources of funds for the program can be listed as:

1) domestic savings – by means of taxation or savings levies;
2) profits from those industries that happen to have a natural comparative advantage in these areas;

3) financial assistance by the advanced members to the under-developed territories. (This is of course, already taking place on a large scale). The Republic of South Africa at present contributes almost all the funds for the administration and development of the Transkei and other Bantu homelands in the Republic. In addition, the South African Government in its 1968 Budget set aside the amount of R5 million for purposes of providing low interest loans for development in neighbouring countries. Mention can also be made of an R8-million loan made by the Republic to Malawi at the low interest rate of 4 per cent;

4) special kinds of fiscal transfers, such as: (a) the revenue at present derived by Botswana, Swaziland and Lesotho from the Republic in terms of the 1910 customs agreement. (This agreement is at present under revision by the various parties concerned). In terms of this agreement the three former "High Commission Territories" each receive small percentages of the gross customs and excise duties (excluding the excise on beverages) accruing to the Republican Treasury, in order to compensate them for the duties on goods consumed by their subjects, and (b) the interest on the "deferred payments" made to miners recruited from these areas by the South African mines. These wages, withheld from the workers while on duty, are payed out to them in their homelands after the expiry of their terms of service. (Specific provision for this system is made, for example, in the agreement between the Republic of South Africa and the government of Portugal under the so-called Moçambique Convention of 1928 as amended in 1964).

Apart from the abovementioned financial flows, several additional sources of development funds can be considered, such as the taxation of labour used in metropolitan areas. Income from this source should be paid over to the authorities in the homelands of these workers. Considering the number of workers from these areas at present employed in the industrial sectors of the Republic, this could be a major source of income to their authorities. Such a tax would at the same time serve the purpose of reducing the comparative cost advantage of location in the metropolitan areas of those industries extensively relying on Bantu labour. The question whether such a tax might simply be shifted on to the consumer would depend on the extent of competition within the particular industry. In those industries where competition is strong, such as the clothing industry, chances are that a certain amount of decentralisation might result. In other cases, such as construction and construction material, employers might be forced to absorb the cost in their industries in which case the income to the homelands would be proportionally larger.

An additional possible source of income to the Bantu homelands, would be a taxation on commodities predominantly consumed by Bantu in metropolitan areas, such as Bantu beer. It would be quite possible to introduce some measure of differentiation in the tax on Bantu beer according to area, so that those Bantu working in the metropolitan areas pay proportionately more than those living in the homelands. In a sense this would introduce a measure of progression in Bantu taxation in view of the fact that the earnings per capita of Bantu in the metropolitan areas are, on the average, several times higher than incomes in the homelands. Moreover, it may be considered to re-allocate a proportion of the profit on Bantu beer, at present devoted to the interests of the Bantu in the Bantu townships in metropolitan areas, to the homelands. At present some municipalities from time to time and on their own initiative pay over a proportion of these profits to the Bantu homelands.

The final and most important form of assistance to these areas by the economically developed Republic, is the creation of infrastructures in advance of the development of industrial superstructures in these areas. The existence and development of an infra-structure, of course, creates certain external economies and cost savings which must normally be financed out of the resources of the community itself. As will be described in the next chapter, it seems very likely that a form of technological integration will result in the sub-continent, from which the under-developed areas should receive a proportionately larger benefit than the costs placed upon them. In fact this expansion of the technological infra-structure over the whole sub-continent would appear to be the most practical point from which the entire programme should be initiated.

The pattern of industrial location and trade which would

result from the programme envisaged above, would partly determine the pattern of infra-structure to be provided throughout the sub-continent as well as the pattern of industrial investment.

Given a *functional* possibility of successful planning, the next problem to be considered is that of *institutional* control. As far as the technological infra-structure is concerned, it seems very likely that the entire programme would have to be tackled by the different governments, as will be described in the next chapter.

As far as the pattern of industrial investment is concerned, it is obvious that private enterprise will undertake some part of this automatically in so far as such action is made economically feasible by the policy instruments of the plan. Private investment has already occurred in the development of the fish industry in South West Africa, mining in Zambia, Rhodesia and Swaziland as well as the citrus and sugar plantations in Rhodesia and the sugar plantations and iron ore mining in Swaziland. The well known Anglo-American Corporation of S.A. has played a leading part in this regard. Its interest even extends into Moçambique (a R1.8 million cashew nut processing plant) while another very large South African group, the General Mining and Finance Corporation, seriously investigated the possibility of oil production and refining in Angola.

As far as the Bantu homelands in the Republic of South Africa are concerned, the issue has for a considerable time been rather confused by the political policy of preventing white capital from entering these areas. As far as we can judge, this was a complete "red herring", for the reason that during the time this policy was adhered to, very little investment opportunities really existed, so that the debate was almost entirely confined to political antagonism. The policy has recently been changed to allow white capital on an agency basis, the implications of which have not yet become quite clear. It would, however, appear that the different development corporations which were and are to be established for the development of the Bantu homelands are to operate as channels through which private White capital and ideas can be turned into development projects. Control will be exercised by the corporations, thus preventing any exploitation.

For all practical reasons, investment in these areas would have to be done in close co-operation with the particular authorities, because of the vital importance to any investment decisions of the special forms of subsidisation.

5. *The present extent of co-operation*

In order to achieve the general object defined in the previous section and to handle the co-ordination of individual decisions regarding the specific objects involved, well defined organs and instruments of co-operation are required. All such specific objects as the redistribution of industrial location and investment according to the "adjusted principles of dynamic comparative advantage", the pattern of labour flows, the financial arrangements and transfers, direct aid, the technological integration of infrastructure and the diffusion of economic and technical knowledge, require a continuous process of decision making and co-ordination.

This kind of co-operation between the several states, may be based on the considerable experiences in the past. Several kinds of agreements and understandings, such as most favoured nations agreements, customs unions, preference agreements, joint marketing arrangements and technological co-operation (such as he now defunct CCTA) have existed between some of the member nations in the sub-continent.

The series of agreements between the Republic of South Africa and the Republic of Portugal in respect of a number of specific objects may, for example, be usefull prototypes in certain instances (Treaty series No. 7, 8, 9, 10, 11 of 1964). The agreement (Treaty series No. 7/1964) in regard to rivers of mutual interest and the Kunene River Scheme, e.g. provide for hydrological co-operation, the use of water and power and the financing of the schemes. The agreement (Treaty series No. 11/1964) regulating the employment of Portuguese workers from Moçambique on certain mines in the Republic, has a similar wider interest. The specific provisions which cover a range of employment conditions, including wages, are less important than the basic principle of negotiation on *inter-governmental* level about the flow of labour. In Treaty No. 10 of 1964, the government of the Republic of South Africa undertakes to secure to the port of Lourenço Marques not less than 40 per cent of the total tonnage of commercial sea borne goods traffic, imported into the "competitive area" (i.e. an area more or less covering the Southern Transvaal). Very similar arrangements have been negotiated with reference to trade relationships with Angola in terms of a 1941 treaty.

Since at present, wages earned by migrant workers from Lesotho in the Republic, constitute the most important single generator of the national income of Lesotho, and feature prominently in many of the other states mentioned, periodic negotiations with the Republican Government would be an important political instrument to improve their "terms of trade" and their share of the final product derived from the employment of these factor services in the sub-continent.

For the Republic, such machinery should provide part of the answers to the problem of Bantu trade unions from which the Republican Government has always withheld the bargaining machinery of the Industrial Conciliation Act, 1956. The position is becoming increasingly embarrassing, but rather than recognise trade unions for foreign workers *within* the Republic's constitutional system, the Government of the Republic of South Africa would probably prefer the inter-governmental negotiation of wages and other terms of employment. Even strikes, in the sense of the with-holding of labour in the absence of agreement, may become part of the instruments of negotiation. In this respect, a great deal of improvement could be brought about in the organisation of Bantu labour migration. At present the Bantu labour market is organised in about 365 municipal labour bureaux and 353 district labour bureaux. Of the district labour bureaux, more than half are situated in or near the Bantu homelands and act as the primary source of supply. The effect of this system at present, is to restrain severely the mobility of Bantu labour between the sources of supply and areas of demand, thus creating monopolistic and monopsonistic positions in each area respectively. The general effect of this system is that much higher wages for the same types of work are negotiated on municipal labour bureau markets than district labour bureau markets, with the result that employers endeavour to avoid the municipal markets, seeking their labour directly in the homelands, while on the other hand, Bantu from the homelands do everything in their power to offer their labour directly on the municipal markets, rather than going through the district markets. A reorganisation of this system in collaboration with the Bantu authorities, in order to concentrate both supply and demand of labour on the district markets in the homelands, seems essential. The effect of this should be the achievement of higher wage levels in the district markets, particularly if it is buttressed by a proposed tax on labour obtained in the metropolitan areas. Eventually therefore, conventions similar to those with Moçambique and Angola could be contemplated with respect to all the other states and emerging states.

Prior to its dissolution on 31st December, 1963, the Federation of the present states of Malawi, Zambia and Rhodesia traded with the Republic of South Africa in terms of fairly comprehensive trade agreements which provided for a number of important mutual trade preferences. Since 1963, normal trade relationships under new agreements have been resumed with Rhodesia (November 1964) and Malawi (March 1967). At the moment, the political tensions with Zambia seem to temporarily preclude a similar approach. With respect to Rhodesia and Malawi, the present political atmosphere for economic cooperation has improved considerably, compared with the situation during the 1950's when these two countries favoured the expansion of trade with the United Kingdom rather than with the Republic.

The trade and monetary union existing between South Africa and the former High Commission Territories (Botswana, Lesotho and Swaziland) since June, 1910, is currently under revision. Under article 2 of the 1910 agreement with the territories the products of the then Union of South Africa and of these territories enjoyed free entry into each others markets, and since then, only spirits, beer and wine were removed from the agreement in 1946. At the same time the Union's external customs tariff became applicable to imports from third countries into the High Commission Territories – a true customs union therefore. In future, however, the target of economic development and growth in these territories would be independently set by their own governments. In consequence it may be doubted whether a full customs union could be continued for very long on the old basis.

Apart from these bilateral agreements between the Republic and other members of the group, several agreements exist among these members themselves. These agreements as is illustrated by Table VI, generally cover the movements of merchandise among these countries.

TABLE VI – ILLUSTRATION OF BILATERAL AGREEMENTS AMONG THE COUNTRIES IN SOUTHERN AFRICA

Country	Republic of South Africa	Botswana, Lesotho and Swaziland	Rhodesia	Malawi	Zambia	Moçam-bique	Angola
Republic of South Africa		X	X	X		X	X
Botswana, Lesotho and Swaziland ...	X						
Rhodesia	X						
Malawi	X					X	X
Zambia							
Moçambique ...	X		X				X
Angola	X		X			X	

As far as marketing is concerned, the products of Botswana, Lesotho and Swaziland are to a very large extent marketed as an integral part of those of South Africa. For example, the South African Citrus Exchange handles the citrus crop of Swaziland as part of the South African crop and markets it under the trade mark of "Outspan". Similarly, in handling wool, the South African Wool Board and Wool Commission do not distinguish between the domestic and Lesotho wool clip, while wool from Lesotho also enjoys the benefit of the South African wool stabilisation scheme. Slaughter stock from Swaziland and beef carcasses from Botswana, are exported to markets in South Africa, subject to veterinary restrictions and administrative considerations to regulate the flow of supply. These products enjoy the advantages of minimum prices per grade and weight which the South African Meat Board guarantees. More such examples could be quoted. In fact, the Minister of Economic Affairs, Mr. J. Haak, some time ago commented that "in this connection South Africa is not unwilling to examine her list of imports in order to establish to what extent she can, within the framework of tariff and trade, offer new or increased markets to the products of countries in Southern Africa even though it is realised that initially their exports will mainly comprise agricultural and to some extent mineral products".

6. *Financial co-operation*

The specific objects of financial co-operation among the members of the system would be (i) national currencies; (ii) international reserves; (iii) money markets; (iv) capital markets; (v) other common financial institutions; and (vi) fiscal management.

The basic question is whether the newly independent states wish to have their own national currencies, rather than foreign currencies, circulating within their own borders. It seems a natural wish from a purely political point of view, but it may have several economic snags.

As long as the central banks of the new states maintain a hundred per cent backing in gold, or in the key currency to which they are tied financially, not much happens economically beyond the incurrence of administrative costs.

Important problems would, however, arise as soon as the governments of Lesotho, Botswana, Rhodesia, or any other member, decided to deviate from the principle of a hundred per cent outside backing of its national currency.

To begin with, an exchange rate problem arises. Since local notes on this basis, would be fully convertible, such convertibility at existing exchange rates would have to be explicitly promised by the national authority. If these governmental undertakings are not accepted by private holders of currencies, the exchange rate would tend to drop, and the governments would have to support it by buying up its own currency in exchange for foreign currencies.

It may, therefore, be economically desirable for any individual country to follow an independent credit policy. At the same time, it clearly implies a number of grave risks for the country itself, and the other members associated with it.

At the moment the various potential members of the system differ widely in this respect. The largest number, i.e., Lesotho, Botswana, Swaziland, the emergent Ovamboland and South West Africa, all use as currency the notes of the South African Reserve Bank. Malawi and Zambia are directly linked with sterling and Angola and Moçambique are in the trade and monetary area of Portugal.

Rhodesia, which used to arrange her payments through the Bank of England, has for the time being naturally made other arrangements.

If closer monetary and financial links within the system of co-operation is to come about in future, the pooling of reserves, would be a matter to consider. Pooling of reserves whether between countries or between companies, implies a very useful conservation of scarce liquid resources.

At the same time it implies an integration of the several systems of exchange control – and would probably in this case also imply the integration of the systems of import control. It would mean, for example, that everyone throughout the area would fall under the same rules governing transfers of money – for example, for buying shares abroad.

In turn, this would probably impose upon each country the need to avoid action which would embarrass the opportunities of other countries to receive money and capital from abroad and to send it abroad.

Thus the chain of reactions in the process of integration is very real. Starting with the pooling of reserves, it ends with the integration of the entire system of economic policy. For this reason, we do not expect any promotion of this idea beyond the integration of the existing economic systems of South Africa, South-West Africa and the former High Commission Territories. Even in this respect, the future may bring changes away from the pooling arrangements.

It might be necessary to come to explicit agreements about the way in which the South African Reserve Bank handles the foreign exchange accounts of these countries now that they may endeavour to follow independent economic policies.

Similarly, the flow of money and capital among members of the system could not be integrated or remain integrated unless the business cycle policies of the various members are integrated under one supra-national body.

Even within South Africa, the approaches to the capital market by municipalities, Escom and other borrowers in the public sector, are co-ordinated on a voluntary basis with the borrowing programme of the central government.

Thus, should Lesotho, Botswana and Swaziland choose to remain financially integrated with South Africa, they might be expected to seek the agreement of the latter government before floating major loans in its market.

In the establishing of these organs and instruments of economic co-operation in the sub-continent, a major matter of principle seems to be the question whether this co-operation should grow out of a series of separately negotiated bilateral agreements between any two members of the group, and in particular between the Republic and any other member on the one hand, or whether, on the other hand, there might be some virtue in the idea of an "Organisation for Economic Co-operation and Development in Southern Africa" roughly on the lines of the prototype created by the countries of Europe. On the face of it such an organisation would certainly improve the image of the idea of co-operation and might contain several other advantages not easily identified such as better co-ordination.

On the other hand, there may be as many practical advantages to the bilateral approach. Most important of these, may be the fact that at present the economic condition and position of each member country differ so much from that of other countries, that it would be very difficult, if not impossible, to arrive at common denominators in multi-lateral agreements. Moreover, the administrative processes of negotiation might be much easier if only two parties to the agreement are involved.

7. *Economic relationships with the rest of the world*
An important aspect of economic co-operation in the sub-continent would be a concerted approach to economic relationships with the rest of the world. Not only would it be extremely difficult in view of the figures quoted, to plan internal trade on the basis of comparative advantages without referring to the nature of the import policies of the various independent regions with regard to the rest of the world, but the effect of rapid growth rates based on industrial diversification on the balance of payments position with each other and with the rest of the world would have to be closely watched. To neglect this aspect in planning programmes would easily render the entire process impractical.

Moreover, this co-operation amongst member countries in their relationships with the rest of the world could be extended also to the infra-structure. A very good example of this is the new international telephone exchange at Cape Town from which a submarine cable connection with Europe is being laid. The cable is one of the greatest projects of this nature ever tackled, and would be the first deep sea long distance cable with a carrying capacity of 360 channels. When it is completed the sub-continent will be in contact with 150 million telephones and 500,000 tele-printers in the rest of the world, with practically no delay. The Rhodesian administration has already indicated that it would rent one of the cable channels while Moçambique would apparently require four. The other administrations still evidently do not have enough traffic to justify the renting of a full cable channel so that the Republic will, as in the past, continue to handle their overseas calls.

CHAPTER III

THE TECHNOLOGICAL REQUISITES OF ECONOMIC CO-OPERATION

Our main interest in the technological infra-structure derives from our arguments in Chapter II, that the improvement of the present industrial advantages of the under-developed members of the sub-continent, and the diversification of their comparative advantages would depend very largely, not only on the "human factor" which is dealt with in Chapter IV but also on the provision of an infra-structure and the creation of external economies for these areas in relation to that of the Republic. In this connection the main interest would settle on the position with regard to transport, communication, tele-communication, power and water supply.

1. *Transport and communication*

A glance at map 2, showing the most important railways, roads and ports, indicates that, as could be expected, the transport structures of the Republic and Rhodesia are by far the best developed on the sub-continent. Thus, for example, Botswana with an area of almost 220,000 square miles, has only one railway line running from Mafeking to Bulawayo through Gaberones at the eastern extremity of the country for 394 miles. On the other hand, Rhodesia with an area of 250,000 square miles, is served by 1,600 miles of railways, traversing the entire territory from Livingstone in the western corner to Rutenga in the south-east and beyond Salisbury in the north. Lesotho leads the rear with only one mile of railway connections within its borders.

On the whole, the motive for the entire railway grid of the sub-continent has been export trade, so that each important railway line is connected with a sea port. Angola provides a very clear example of this, with 1,800 miles of track distributed over four different and independent railway systems, unconnected with each other. Even in the Republic of South Africa, the vast system of more than 12,000 miles, over an area of 472,000 square miles, has been built mainly to connect the mineral deposits of

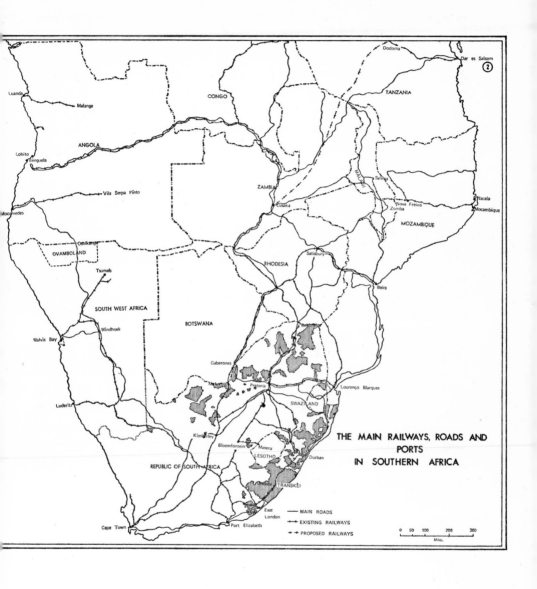

THE MAIN RAILWAYS, ROADS AND
PORTS
IN SOUTHERN AFRICA

—— MAIN ROADS
+—+ EXISTING RAILWAYS
+—+ PROPOSED RAILWAYS

0   50   100   200   300
|__|__|__|_____|_____|
                Miles.

the Transvaal interior with the ports of Cape Town and Durban.

The railway line between Lourenço Marques and Johannesburg, was also mainly justified on these grounds. The reason for the pattern of railway connections was the economic and political power struggle around the turn of the century. Had the area been a single political entity, it seems doubtful whether the pattern of lines would have been laid along the same routes. A glaring example of this historical development, is the fact that Rhodesia is to-day directly connected by railway through Gabarones, Mafeking and De Aar with Cape Town, completely by-passing its natural interior market of the Southern Transvaal, which was controlled at that time, by the politically hostile government of Paul Kruger. Thus, the lack of political co-operation (grantedly quite impossible in those days) and the emphasis upon the export of primary products, resulted in a railway network which seems completely inadequate for intra-regional economic co-operation and trade.

Even at present most new important expansions of railway transport still emphasise this connection with ports and exports towards the rest of the world, an understandable position in the light of the very large dependence on trade with the rest of the world shown in Chapter II. Thus, the system is almost completely "port directed" rather than "region-directed", with the result that the famous distance barrier to trade has been broken down with the rest of the world rather than with member states of the group. The major expansion schemes at present beyond the blue print stage are new connections between Mpinde in Malawi and the Moçambique port of Nacala, and between Ndola in Zambia and Dar-es-Salaam the main port of Tanzania. Although it may be true that substantial and profitable two way trade will only grow if the gap in the development level between the trading partners is continuously narrowed, a functional relationship may exist the other way round: to the extent that the distance barriers among the internal regions are perhaps artificially broken down, the basis will be laid for the narrowing of the gap in development level.

Thus the linking up of the four functionally separate railway lines in Angola, would be an example of an effort to stimulate internal economic activity. Other possible ideas for furthering inter-regional railway communications, would be the linking of the Angola railway system with that of South Africa up to Tsumeb, the linking of both South West Africa and Botswana with the Southern Transvaal from Gobabis to Gaberones and further west, and finally the linking of the Rhodesian system from West Nicholson in the south of Rhodesia with Beit Bridge in the Northern Transvaal. This latter link, has been considered by a recent commission appointed by the Rhodesian Government and has already been initiated. Since the Rhodesian network is well linked up with Lusaka in Zambia and Beira in Moçambique and at least in principle connected with Lobito-Bay along the Benguela railway which runs also through the Congo, the West Nicholson – Beit Bridge connection would have considerable economic advantages for inter-territorial trade. Also, in the light of the development of the Kunene project which will be discussed below, the Tsumeb connection seems to be a natural outcome and even the Gobabis-Gabarones connection might become an economic proposition particularly if coupled with the harnessing of the irrigation potential of the Okavango at the northern extremity of the territory.

On the other hand, the inter-territorial transport connections required might be more economically provided by road. Again, the Republic and Rhodesia are at present far and way best served. Actually, the inter-territorial connections are considerably superior in this respect than those by rail, as is shown in map 2 depicting the main tarred roads on the sub-continent. The economics of substitution in respect of rail and road transport are extremely complicated. Whilst it is true that the cost per mile of laying a tarred road, is considerably less than that of laying a railway line, the carrying capacity of the latter would off-set the cost difference to a considerable extent. In practice very much, obviously, depends on the nature of the goods to be transported. At the moment, many of the products are primary commodities suitable for bulk haulage, but as development proceeds the need for rapid transportation in small units may become of major importance. Several extensions are indeed already being planned. Thus, a new tarred road is being built from Otjiwarongo in the north of South West Africa to Ruacana in Southern Angola which connection will link with a tarred road to Luanda, completing the pattern of a vast development project between the Republic of South Africa and Angola.

As far as the identified Bantu homelands in the Republic are concerned, most of them are fairly well served with both rail and road links, particularly in the sense that the South African Railways provide a road transport service from the few railway sidings to the interior. Some of these roads used by the railway buses are however still in need of considerable improvement in quality. In the case of the Transkei, a railway line has been in existence for many years specifically to serve the needs of this area.

As far as human traffic, in respect of both the transport of workers and the movement of entrepreneurs, officials and other leaders of economic development are concerned, a very well developed air transport system exists, and is developing very rapidly between most of the areas concerned. This service may in future become one of the main ways in which the vast tourist potential of these areas could be exploited.

Similar conditions obtained with regard to tele-communication services between the various areas of the group. Again the internal network of the Republic, South West Africa and Rhodesia are vastly superior to those of the other territories. As against the 1.6 telephones per thousand inhabitants in operation in 1965 in Lesotho, 68.6 telephones per thousand inhabitants were available in the Republic, 40.9 in South West Africa and 22.5 in Rhodesia. The position was little better in Zambia with 8.6 telephones installed per thousand people.

These statistical differences do not necessarily reflect a lack of communication *between* the various areas, but indicate more particularly the extent to which each community is internally linked. It seems clear that inter-territorial communications already exist and should not present a serious barrier to the development of trade and economic activities generally between these areas.

In any case, the inter-territorial network certainly seems superior to that existing in the rest of Africa, and the importance of this type of communication for the developing countries is fully realised. Evidence of this is the conference on tele-communication administration in Southern Africa held in July, 1967, in Pretoria.

The conference was attended by representatives from the Republic, Botswana, Lesotho, Moçambique, Rhodesia, Swaziland and South West Africa. At this conference, it was agreed to maintain the present operator-to-subscriber dialling procedure, with a view to switching over to more modern systems in the foreseeable future. As far as telegraph systems are concerned, a basis was laid at this conference for the eventual integration of the automatic telegraph and telex systems of the Republic and those of neighbouring states. In this way, the Republic will enable these states to communicate with each other directly.

2. *Water and power*

It is in the generation and use of power that the main theme of this chapter emerges most clearly. The idea of co-operation which would be advantageous to all of the members of the group enabling the Republic to lower its cost structure and providing the underdeveloped areas with a means to bring about an effective take-off has recently been widely advocated by Dr. H. J. van Eck, one of South Africa's foremost industrial leaders and, inter alia, chairman of the board of directors of the Industrial Development Corporation. In one of his many explanations of his ideas, Van Eck said: "We can make electricity the most important single interlinking factor in Southern Africa. If we really want to help our neighbours, these are the lines along which we must direct our thinking. We can help them to overcome one of the greatest problems that baulk the economic growth of less-developed countries, namely, the fact that without the price advantages of large-scale production they cannot take-off".

The Republic's power grid, is based on thermal electricity (which relies on the use of coal and water) radiated from a complex of pithead stations spread across the coal fields of the Southern Transvaal. According to Professor D. C. Midgley (upon whose professional knowledge the following paragraphs are mainly based) some of the largest single thermal stations in the world are already being planned as components of that complex. The whole of the Republic's power needs for many decades into the future can without doubt, be derived from this central power complex, within which the capacity of plant under construction or being planned already totals 10,000 MW and which will increase

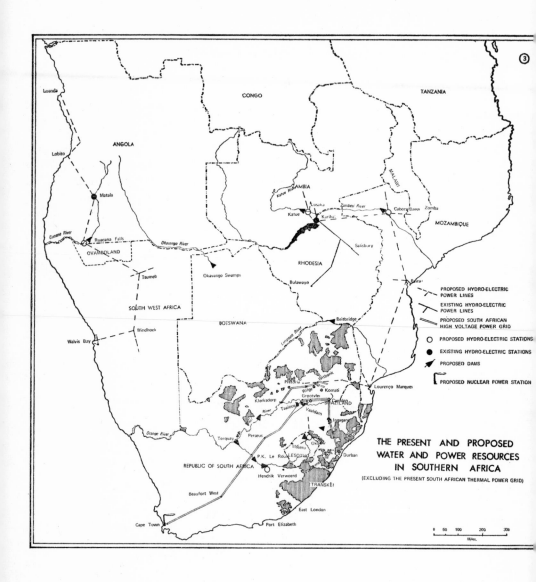

③

THE PRESENT AND PROPOSED
WATER AND POWER RESOURCES
IN SOUTHERN AFRICA

(EXCLUDING THE PRESENT SOUTH AFRICAN THERMAL POWER GRID)

PROPOSED HYDRO-ELECTRIC
POWER LINES

EXISTING HYDRO-ELECTRIC
POWER LINES

PROPOSED SOUTH AFRICAN
HIGH VOLTAGE POWER GRID

○ PROPOSED HYDRO-ELECTRIC STATIONS

● EXISTING HYDRO-ELECTRIC STATIONS

▶ PROPOSED DAMS

PROPOSED NUCLEAR POWER STATION

0   50   100   200   300
Miles.

rapidly to more than 50,000 MW by the close of the century. Taking the short to middle term view, it would therefore appear as if the Republic could "go it alone" as far as its power supply is concerned, but, while the coal supply would probably be sufficient, there is no doubt that such a strategy would place a severe burden on the limited water supplies of the Republic.

On the other hand, in the Portuguese province of Angola, controlling the vast water resources of the Kunene, most of the electric power generated is from hydro sources, but only a minor fraction of the potential has been developed. Few of the schemes established provide surplus power, because they were built below potential, owing to the lack of demand. Similarly, if the development of the equally vast water resources of the river Zambesi in the Portuguese province of Moçambique, is to be economically feasible, projects must be undertaken on a grand scale. It will, however, be many decades before Moçambique itself will be able to absorb such quantities of energy. It was therefore clear to the Portuguese that if they could persuade the Republic to enter into a contract to purchase a substantial proportion of the energy surplus the full potential of these schemes in Angola and Moçambique could be developed economically and the resulting revenue would enable them to tackle the land reclamation and irrigation projects without which they would find difficulty in raising their agricultural productivity to the take-off levels. (Hydro-electric energy is most economically produced within the framework of the multi-purpose project).

Even in some of the Bantu homelands such possibilities exist. Looked at from the direct economic point of view the Republican authorities could argue that they need not bother with such hydro-electric power development because the factories are relatively small and the unit cost of energy higher than that from the coal fields complex. On the other hand, Professor Midgley argued "how can the agricultural development of the Transkei, for instance, be advanced without the revenue that could be derived from its own water resources and from the development which its water projects would initiate?" Similarly, Lesotho, lying to the south east of the Vaal Basin, and over a short distance contiguous with it, would probably never use more than a small percentage of her very considerable supplies of water which could be linked with the Vaal Dam, the water reservoir of 90 per cent of the industrial complex in the Southern Transvaal.

The Republican authorities have, however, chosen the "outward looking" strategy. South Africa has agreed to take part of the output from the Matala station on the Kunene for use in the Tsumeb mines of South West Africa. From Tsumeb the line will eventually link up with Usakos and Windhoek in the south and from Usakos another line will branch off to Swakopmund and Walvis Bay. As part of the same scheme, some water is to be drawn from the Kunene for the development of Ovamboland.

Negotiations between the Republic and the Portuguese authorities for the development of the Cabora Bassa hydro-electric project on the Zambesi are in an advanced stage. Negotiations with Lesotho for the use of power and water from the projected Oxbow Lake Scheme have reached the final stage.

All these schemes, as well as the Electricity Supply Commission's giant thermal power station in the Eastern Transvaal, the planned nuclear power station to be built in the Western Cape, together with further developments of the potential of the Kariba dam, drafted on to the existing thermal power grid of the Electricity Supply Commission (Escom) constitute a vast integrated network spreading over the entire sub-continent. At present, practical thinking has to exclude Zambia for political reasons, but the inclusion of the Kariba scheme into the grid and the greater economic activity and demand for power might make possible the further development of the North Bank station of the Kariba scheme.

In such an integrated scheme a measure of supra-national control would have to be accepted. Individually none of these schemes however large some of them may be (the potential of the proposed Cabora Bassa component alone is about 60 per cent of the the Republic's current annual energy demand), would seriously embarrass the Republic from a control point of view. The power output from the Oxbow scheme would be small compared with the enormous capacity of the Escom system, and the load could immediately be taken up by its large thermal capacity.

However, from a cost point of view the Republic would gain considerably – all of these schemes could supply the Republic with power at a lower cost per unit than that at present incurred by its thermal processes, even considering the tremendous distances over which this power has to be transmitted. The considerable improvements in the modern high tension DC transmission methods will make this possible.

The territories involved, especially those feeding power into the grid, would increase their national incomes by very significant proportions. In the case of Lesotho, for example, the value of the output of power could contribute roughly a third of the country's whole export income. In other cases this figure would be less, but still very significant. In addition, the availability of low cost electricity supply would, for all the underdeveloped areas, be a most important determinant of their take-off possibility into industrial diversification.

The generation of hydro-electric power is both technologically and economically closely linked up with the availability and the further use of water. From the Oxbow Lake, the sub-continent would not only receive a supply of electricity, but the Vaal Basin would also be supplemented with a considerable supply of water. Another important source of water in the sub-continent is the Okavango, a major river system which dissipates itself in a vast swamp at the northern extremity of Botswana and which cannot be economically harnessed except on a grand scale. Botswana's present needs, however, do not warrant large scale development works and so the country is obliged to struggle with scattered, sub-economic, single purpose, minor schemes while its principle resources lie dormant.

In this connection, Professor Midgley had in mind, a multi-purpose international scheme which would drain portions of the Okavango swamps in Botswana for agricultural purposes, supply water for irrigating the Renoster Valley of the Republic "North-West of the Orange Free State Goldfields" and distribute water to the Witwatersrand complex and later to other existing and potential demand centres. Moreover, since water from the Okavango would have to be pumped, the linking of the power networks by way of a transmission line across Botswana to the Transvaal, rather than through South West Africa to the North-Western Cape, would, according to Midgley, offer attractive advantages, particularly for Botswana.

The prospect of water from the Okavango would also alter current planning to the advantage of South Africa's neighbours to the East, namely Swaziland and Moçambique. To supply the Republic's pithead power stations, appreciable quantities of water will have to be drawn from the Komati and Usutu rivers which flow into Swaziland and onwards into Moçambique. Although these rivers receive considerable augmentation from the high rain fall areas within Swaziland, the possibility of a reduction in the quantities abstracted within the Republic would certainly be attractive to the Republic's neighbours.

In Chapter II we have distinguished between the problems of the control of industry on the one hand and the problems of location of industry on the other. With respect to the creation of infra-structure the same kind of problem arises: given the functional nature of the transport, tele-communication, water and power networks, would it be possible to allow the same kind of atomistic, individual, or even state control of small projects, relying on a system of periodic or sporadic consultation and negotiation for the necessary co-operation on the functional level, or would the economics as well as the technology of the infra-structure require a greater measure of integration of control?

The basic point of departure for our thesis in general, was that the maximum measure of political sovereignty would, for the foreseeable future, have to be maintained and even developed among the various identified states in the group. It is unnecessary to repeat the reasons for this point of departure which was discussed fully in Chapter I, but as our arguments developed, it became clear that this political sovereignty could not be maintained on the basis of economic and technological isolation. Since, full integration in the sense of relinquishing control over the functional participation in trade, finance and communication would also destroy this idea of self-determination, we have suggested the principle of co-operation which was defined as that system in which each participating member would still retain control over the nature and extent of his participation in the system. Our examination of the facts so far, has led us to the conclusion that the field of such separate control would have to be limited somewhat. As far as agricultural developments are concerned, the various individual members would have to face the fact that land is at present their most important source of wealth and it would have to be conserved according to the most economical principles of exploitation. For example, in order to reap most benefits from agriculture, certain kinds of land reform and agricultural techniques would have to be adopted which might lead to *less* total employment in agriculture than might have been desired by the states in order to retain their populations within their own borders. Thus, political control of employment becomes confined to secondary and tertiary sectors. In these fields, it is important to stimulate private enterprise and the profit motive. The nature of industrialisation, particularly if extensive methods or processes of production are resorted to, would be such that various alternative patterns might be fairly equally feasible. Many possible different patterns of industrial structure would be possible within certain cost margins. This brings us to the infra-structure services. Here again, the extent of political sovereignty would have to be severely limited by the technological nature of the processes. The cost difference between small micro units of power generation, irrigation projects and tele-communication systems, railway connections and even roads, on the one hand, and that of the giant units considered in this chapter, on the other hand would be such that the political authorities would, economically speaking, have very little choice between the one and the other. If their take-off into sustained industrial growth should materialize in practice, and a measure of self-respecting and satisfying political self-determination is to be achieved in this sphere, sovereignty would have to be re-linquished in the field of technological co-operation. In this way, our thesis has developed into (1) *technological integration,* (2) *economic co-operation particularly in the industrial field,* and (3) *political independence.*

It seems that the way to avoid that the efforts of very small nations to decide things for themselves lapse into a negative process of disintegration, is to establish practical systems of economic co-operation on the levels of both private initiative and government planning. The smaller the individual communities, the greater the need for co-operation.

CHAPTER IV

THE SOCIOLOGICAL FRAMEWORK

Even if the technological requisites for an economically profitable system of mutual co-operation should prove to be ideal, the possibility exists that the various peoples may not be able, or in a position to exploit the opportunities for the functional co-operation envisaged in Chapter II. Economists have come to refer to these limitations as "the human factor", but in order to avoid the *a priori* conception that these limitations emanate from the innate attitudes of the individual subject in the communities of Southern Africa, we would prefer to use the term "sociological framework" in its broadest conception to embrace the entire complex of man made institutions, from the unwritten mores to the written constitutions, which have a bearing on the ability of these communities to exploit their economic opportunities and to maintain a minimum of political and administrative stability for this purpose.

1. *The social will and ability to economise*

From the economist's point of view, it is not directly material whether economic opportunities are exploited by individuals of these communities as independent actors, or by the communities collectively under some system of communal decision making, provided it is the most efficient system of decision making under the circumstances.

In this connection economics as a profession has come under the rather severe suspicion of other social sciences, particularly political theory and anthropology, but the suspicion surely rests on a misconception of the function of economics as a discipline of thought.

Economists have indeed maintained that the processes of economic development and growth are universal, everywhere the same, but that various communities in the world find themselves in different stages of this process, possibly for sociological reasons, but there may be a whole combination of other limitations. The economic principle does not maintain that such sociological institutions as do obtain in economically retarded communities must be scrapped in favour of western patterns. There may well be sociological systems which could accommodate the economic principle as well (although history has not yet produced many examples!)

In as much as it is up to the technologist to devise means of improving communications along lines that fit in with the natural circumstances of Southern Africa, it seems up to sociologists (in the broad sense) to similarly treat the human institutions of Southern Africa.

The historiography of this matter goes back at least to the nineteenth century sociologist, Max Weber, whose thesis that the protestant ethic was mainly responsible for the rapid progress of the Germanic cultures along the path of economic growth, became classical, if not necessarily completely acceptable. Equally influential as a general approach became A. Toynbee's theory of "challenge and response". Similarly well-known are the themes of Arthur Lewis on "the will to economise", W. Rostow on the "preconditions of development in the traditional society" and Hirschman's "latent entrepreneurial potential", et cetera.

We will therefore assume that the path of economic development is indeed a universal matter, and that the practical thing to do is to identify those aspects of retarded communities which inhibit their progress along this path. If it should turn out that to grow economically a culture would have to destroy its basic identity, the community would have a clear but stark choice indeed.

For the nations in our study, however, this stark choice would not arise. We know of no authority on culture who maintains such a thesis for any of these nations. On the contrary, an increasing number of scholars of the South African Bantu, for example, are insisting that a very great proportion of the economically inhibiting behavioural patterns followed by Bantu peoples are not at all essential to their cultural identity. According to this point of view, it is not necessary to become a European to be able to exploit economic opportunities.

The decisions could be made individually or collectively. There are, even in principle, strong arguments in favour and against both; no panacea for ideal growth exists and it is futile to seek it. In Western society, the assumption that decentralized decision

65

making produces economically superior results has prevailed for at least the last two centuries, although increasing fields of action in which collective values override individual values have been accepted. In African communities, sociologists have created a presumption against the individual as an economic dynamic decision maker.

Generalisations, however, necessary, should be qualified.

The several communities within the Southern African framework differ very greatly from each other in their possession of these characteristics. The greatest differences, are obviously found between the European community of the Republic, on the one hand, and the Bantu speaking communities as a group, on the other hand. It would be a mistake, however, to assume that either the Whites or the Bantu are homogeneous in this respect. The most casual observer would notice vast differences between the business community of a Bantu Township such as Soweto, on the one hand, and most inhabitants of a rural homeland district such as Sibasa in the Northern Transvaal.

It seems self-evident from the differences in activity between the Sowetan and the rural Pedi, for example, that, in so far as the "human factor" is a retarding element in the process of growth, this is due in greater measure to *environment* than to *innate attitudes*. This viewpoint is little more than a hypothesis, and does not rest on proof.

It has been established empirically that people from rural "homelands" in South Africa, are able to adopt the "western work ideology" within a single generation if placed in the required environment. Other studies also indicate that Bantu farmers, for example, become more sensitive to marketing possibilities and price changes once they are in closer communication with these matters. Nevertheless, not much more should be claimed for these observations than the point that improving the environment is a *necessary condition* for the development of the individual. (It may not be a sufficient condition).

There have always been exceptions to the general presumption that the decision making entity among the Bantu peoples is the tribe under a chieftain with the advice of his councillors, and within the bounds of tradition.

Thus the witchdoctor, in practice, stood outside the sanctions of the community and often displayed a great deal of enterprise and innovation. He in particular was singularly prepared to accept personal responsibility for the implications of his own decisions – an essential characteristic of the capitalistic entrepreneur.

Another exception may be the migrant to the cities. On the whole migration to the cities is today regarded as an integral part of the young Bantu's introduction into maturity and has largely filled the gap caused by the decline of militarism. Consequently the trek to the cities becomes a challenge every young man must face.

This channel is, however, also seized upon by the men who feel themselves too inhibited by the equalisation and collectivation imposed upon them by the tribal way of life. It is among these men, that individualism may develop and who, in their own societies may face the problem of greater limitations on their freedom of action than they may feel prepared to accept.

The communal norms are most comprehensive in the traditional forms of economic activity on the land. In mining, too, several communities have collectively refused to work underground. But in industrial and commercial activities the force of tradition and of the chieftain is weaker.

On the other hand, it is an interesting fact that the Bantu workers in industry have excelled in lines which bear a reasonably close resemblance to the basic knowledge of their communities. Thus, they have rapidly been inducted into textile and clothing factories, construction units, furniture factories, the food and beverage industries, etc., but less in the engineering and printing industry. In transport, they have proved themselves to be efficient drivers on cranes, bull-dozers, etc., and even on heavy duty vehicles where they have eagerly learned the techniques of the jobs. On the other hand, their road sense is low – a discipline completely absent in their own communities.

As far as the trading function is concerned, there seems to be very little in the Bantu cultures which would inhibit the growth of modern money techniques out of the primitive barter systems. Sophisticated trading on own account as an individual entrepreneur may be inhibited by a difficulty to apply the consistency and responsibility to abstract concepts required by modern accounting systems and financial techniques. On the other hand, the concept of personal contractual liability, although not cast in terms of European jurisprudence, is strongly developed. Even the basic idea of interest long denied in the European culture of the middle ages, is firmly accepted among the Bantu.

On the whole, individualism among the Bantu may be unduly inhibited by the attitude of the average person that to maintain and protect his collective rights in the community (e.g. working a piece of land) he is automatically bound to accept collective responsibilities which may be purely imaginary and not at all part of the basic laws of his community. For a break-through of the freedom of decision, a greater degree of clarity on the difference between meaningless habits and basic cultural responsibilities would be singularly effective.

These considerations, incidentally, provide an additional argument in favour of the expansion of industrial and commercial activities. Since the inhibiting traditions of society are more particularly present in agricultural pursuits, the chances are that outside agriculture a more rapid evolution towards some national system of motives and principles could be developed *de novo*.

Whether focussed on the individual, the tribe, or the nation, the main problem seems to be the achievement of a balance between environmental improvements and cultural values. Many examples exist of the destruction of buildings and the decay of other assets provided for or transplanted into a community who reject these objects as harmful, or ignore them as valueless.

On the other hand, one of the main criticisms levelled against the traditional system of Bantu education (administered by non-Bantu authorities) has been its irrelevance to the environment in which the products of these schools are expected to function.

The dilemma is clear. Unless the people are educated to value the material elements of a dynamic society, they might reject them; on the other hand, unless the environment exists, there is little incentive for the community to adapt its cultural values accordingly.

The answer may appear to be a "balanced programme" of education and environmental improvements. Unfortunately, the search for exact balance too often leads to the zero co-ordinate where everything is "in balance", but nothing really exists!

Some unbalance between motivation, on the one hand, and

the pattern of abilities and competences, on the other hand, seems quite unavoidable. These lags, one way or the other, may even be a necessary condition for the process of cultural adaptation. Lags which produce conflict, also produce the action without which change is impossible.

Provided these lags between individual motivation and general environment are not too large, our impression, shared by many economists and sociologists with experience among the Bantu, is that adaptations will be intelligent and not negatively rejective. The traditional sector will adapt itself to environment without eruption. Belief in traditional methods will more easily give way to demonstratively more efficient experimental methods than many philosophies on traditionalism imply. On the other hand, the individualist pioneer, with a motivational spirit well ahead of his community will hardly turn to perverse exploits such as subversion where his ambitions may in principle be satisfied in time.

In any case, the peoples of Southern Africa have no alternative but to seek economic development along these lines of step-by-step change – i.e. by the lagged interaction of motivation and environment, with the lead oscillating from the one element to the other.

For this reason, we do not favour the idea of holding back all action until some "grand blueprint" for balanced growth on all fronts has been drafted in the offices of government departments by the large departmental committees so commonly resorted to by modern governments. These committees can do useful work, but change cannot, and should not, have to await the "final results" of their deliberations. "Sufficient unto the day is the problems thereof".

If our basic political assumption is upheld that the nations of Southern Africa should be defined on a *de jure* basis, i.e., including within each nation all its people irrespective of their present geographical location, there can be no doubt that the will to act economically is ahead of the opportunities to act economically. The lagging element at present is environment.

2. *The administrative structure*

As was described in Chapter I, the communities involved in our discussions, present an extremely heterogeneous pattern of different degrees of political autonomy.

These differences range from complete autonomy in economic affairs in the case of Malawi and Zambia to the semi-independence enjoyed by the newly emerging Bantu authorities in the Republic. Lesotho, Botswana and Swaziland, although recognised as politically independent, are economically still integral parts of the Southern African customs and monetary union. The constitutional position of Rhodesia remains at the time of writing at a problematic stage whilst Angola and Moçambique are official provinces of a European power.

This heterogeneity necessarily seriously complicates the process of co-ordination on administrative level. The Republican practice of bilateral rather than multi-lateral negotiation, whatever the ultimate advantages the latter approach may contain, seems to be an inevitable approach at the present stage.

This political heterogeneity is to a certain extent also reflected in the diversity of the domestic administration. In the case of the Portuguese provinces, Rhodesia and of course the Republic of South Africa, a long standing European tradition of administration exists. In the remaining cases Bantu functionaries had to be rapidly appointed and promoted into occupations previously held by Europeans, although this process has taken place much more gradually than further north of the 6th parallel. The only possible exception may be Zambia, where a more militant process of Africanisation is taking place. In Lesotho and Malawi rapid planning of new state departments is being undertaken with some cautious assistance from South Africa. In the South African Bantu homelands, the tribal chieftains and their councillors traditionally were endowed with a certain power over the activities of their tribesmen, but as a result of the large scale migration of their subjects, and the changing demands of more modern forms of activity, these powers became less relevant to present day conditions, and rapidly disintegrated.

The Republican Governtment's approach, as for example embodied in the Bantu Authorities Act (No. 68 of 1951) is to grant *official* recognition, not only to their existence and traditional powers, but also to lay down a number of definite new functions relating to the need for the development of new activities, including economic expansion.

Thus the chieftain of a tribe now is officially endowed with important powers of legal administration, public health, soil conservation and rehabilitation, and the utilisation of labour resources (including the administration of Bantu labour bureaux).

It may, accordingly be accepted that, at least in agricultural pursuits (including area planning) the position of these chieftains as the communal decision making entities will be considerably strengthened.

This approach, in the circumstances prevailing, may have considerable merit. The administration of technical assistance by South African advisers in the Republican Government can be much more effective if concentrated on a small number of leaders, rather than dissipated over the entire population of peasant farmers, a large number of whom, will, in any case not react without the consent of their chief.

The success of this approach, of course, depends very largely on the subjective attitudes of these tribal chiefs towards dynamic evolution, particularly in economic affairs. A disturbing element of this approach may be the fact that these chiefs come into their authority by succession rather than election, or appointment on personal merit. Consequently, many cases of refusal to co-operate, excessive conservatism, direct opposition and lethargy are indeed encountered.

Efforts to overcome these inhibiting motives and attitudes are, however, made, for example in the special schools set up in all the Bantu homelands, for the training of future tribal chiefs in their responsibilities. Ultimately, too, a chief, who blatantly and continuously, disregards the advice of his councillors and the interests of his tribe, may be deposed by his people in various ways, or officially deprived of his powers of authority.

This system retains much more decisional decentralisation than might appear superficially. Although the ultimate national entities will be the eight territorial authorities, in the Tswana, Ciskei, North Sotho areas, etc. (from which the more independent states of which the Transkei Government is the present prototype, will arise) economically important decisions are in fact taken by the more than 500 tribal chiefs and their councillors within the territories of these national entities.

A final problem, confined to the Bantu homelands emerging from the Republic of South Africa, concerns the applicability in these homelands, of the Republican system of state control over economic activity.

This system is largely contained in statutes such as the Wage Act of 1957, the Factories, Machinery and Buildings Work Act of 1941, the Shops and Offices Act of 1964, the Industrial Conciliation Act of 1956, The Workmen's Compensation Act of 1941, the Unemployment Insurance Act of 1946. These Acts lay down certain minimum standards of wages, fringe benefits and other labour conditions in the Republic. They have been conceived largely with the Western industrialised and highly urbanised society in mind. Many of the requirements in these statutes are either too stringent, or irrelevant in the more primitive circumstances of the homelands. Moreover, their effect on the cost of labour per unit of output may be an important impediment to the creation of comparative cost advantages in these areas. This is underlined by the fact that in the already completely independent states of Malawi, Lesotho, etc., these South African standards do not apply. There are, however, indications that the Republican Government is contemplating the necessary statutory differentiation in this regard.

A broader problem, relevant to this issue, is the statutory responsibility of the Republican Government for the general economic policy of the entire area, including the homelands. There is no indication as yet, that the statutory position in this regard will also be differentiated so that the Transkei, for example, would have the same powers to isolate itself from, for example, an excessively deflationary or excessively protective policy of the Republican authorities.

These problems of statutory economic control will become of increasing importance as comparisons between for example the Transkei and Lesotho or Malawi, are made, and particularly if Malawi is seen to gain certain net advantages from its greater degree of political independence in this regard.

It is indeed on this level of the differentiated social framework in South Africa that the thesis of political independence and economic co-operation will become of increasing relevance.